HOW TO ASSESS YOUR MANAGERIAL STYLE

HOW TO ASSESS YOUR MANAGERIAL STYLE

Charles Margerison

A Division of
AMERICAN MANAGEMENT ASSOCIATIONS

To the sisters
Flo, Doris, Ada, Violet,
and their brothers

Library of Congress Cataloging in Publication Data

Margerison, Charles
  How to assess your managerial style.

  1. Management—Evaluation—Problems, exercises, etc.
I. Title.
HD58.9.M37 1980   658.4'013   80-66867
ISBN 0-8144-5632-4

First published in 1979 by MCB Publications Limited,
Bradford, West Yorkshire, England.

© 1979 MCB Human Resources Limited.

Published in the United States in 1980 by AMACOM,
a division of American Management Associations, New York.
All rights reserved. Printed in the United States of America.

First Printing

Preface

THIS BOOK is for those who wish to question what they do and how they do it. It is particularly written for those in leadership positions. I have spent many hours discussing with managers their work and the task of getting things done. Managers have invariably emphasized the importance of knowing more about themselves and the people with whom they work.

The ideas I have put together here form the basis for a dialogue—both with yourself and with others. The issues identified come from my own interests and those of the managers with whom I have worked.

Let us, however, be clear right from the beginning about one thing. The exercises given in this book are not tests. They are vehicles to start a debate. They have not been subjected to rigorous analysis for validity or reliability. That remains to be done by those who wish to develop them for scientific use. My purpose here is purely that of personal insight. I have used them in management education workshops and find they are an aid in stimulating a real and lively debate about key issues in leadership and managerial work.

So that is how I see this book being used. The scores suggest ways for you to consider your own job, your meetings, your leadership style, your organization, and other aspects of work life. They give you an opportunity to examine your current situation and provide a basis for a similar

dialogue with other colleagues. I believe if this book stimu-
lates such dialogue it will have achieved its purpose.

This is a do-it-yourself book. It is written for people who
have a practical approach to their work but wish to understand more about some of the factors underlying what they
do, so they can improve. This is a book for those interested
in understanding and improving their approach to their
jobs. It emphasizes key aspects of managerial effectiveness.
I hope that positive action will follow your personal analysis.

My thanks to June Wardill, who not only typed and re-
typed the manuscript but kept me organized and on track
in a most friendly way.

I suppose most of the ideas in this book have been tried
out in various ways with my own very personal management
team—the Margerison family. Managing a family is probably harder work all around than managing in an organization. In this I have learned from my wife, Colinette, how it
can be done with humor, care, and a lot of love.

I guess managing should be fun. I have certainly enjoyed
writing this book. I hope it will be relevant for you in your
managerial role. I trust it will also be relevant for my children Jill, Alan, Colinette Ann, and John Paul, when they
take on responsibilities similar to ours.

Charles Margerison

Contents

Discover your approach to leadership

DISCOVER YOUR APPROACH TO LEADERSHIP

WHAT SORT OF LEADER ARE YOU? We will assume that as you are reading this book you already occupy a position of leadership or are in the process of becoming a leader. Each of us has a different way of managing work and in particular managing the work of other people. For our purposes we shall define the leader as one who is responsible for managing the work of other people. Naturally, a major part of this is the way in which the leader manages himself and his own time.

Many people have asked, "Is there a best style of leadership?" There have been numerous attempts at trying to identify the characteristics of effective and ineffective leaders, but so far no one style has been found to be effective in all situations. The task is to identify the approach that you currently employ and look at its effectiveness in the context of your job. The emphasis here will be to concentrate on developing leadership strengths. To do this it is important to know a substantial amount about your own aptitudes, interests, and preferred ways of working. Each person has his own individual way of doing things. In order to become successful, it is important to build upon the particular strengths that one has and at the same time minimize the areas of weakness.

A key question therefore is, "Can leaders be trained?" There is a common assumption that leaders can be developed. This stands in contradiction to the original view that leaders "are born and not made." This view was certainly held in the days of the aristocracy and when opportunities were very limited for people to advance beyond the position that they had been given in society as a result of their birth. Today of course with wider educational opportunity, it is assumed that leaders can be developed and we need not rely entirely upon people reaching leadership position simply on being born into particular families.

However, it is clear from research that the way we approach our life and work is determined by many factors. For example, intelligence to a large extent is inherited. It can be influenced to a slight extent by training but a substantial part of it is taken from the genes of our parents. Of all the factors that have been identified in leadership research, it is clear that intelligence is a central factor which influences leadership ability. Therefore, if we have not been fortunate in inheriting a certain degree of intelligence it is unlikely that we will succeed in a number of key leadership roles and that our level in an organization will be regulated by this factor. However, beyond this there are many factors we can influence, given our interests and abilities.

There is now a considerable body of information which suggests that the way we approach work is determined by certain interests or dispositions. For example, some people like to work with machines and things whereas other people prefer to work with theories and ideas. It would seem that these preferences are something which develop early in our life and stay with us over a considerable period of time. They will therefore influence the sort of leadership positions that we will take on.

Clearly, there need to be different levels of leadership ability in a hierarchy. Also there needs to be a wide range of leadership skill in tackling different jobs. For example, is it likely that the man who will make a good leader of a research team will also make a good leader of the sales force? Is it likely that the man who will become an excellent leader of a football team will also make a first-class manager in a factory? Do you think that the man who makes an effective headmaster of a school would make an equally good leader of a company producing food products or indeed as manager of a group of shops? The wide variety of skills and abilities that are required in various leadership jobs I believe shows that we need many different kinds of leaders. This again flies in the face of previous theories which suggest that a leader once identified can manage virtually any situation. It was originally the view, certainly in Civil Service jobs, that a leader could move from department to department, organizing the work of people involved. Now this may be true, but if it is, then I would suggest that it is because the nature of those jobs and the people involved were relatively similar. The situation in the world at large is that the types of leaders that we require vary considerably because of the nature of the tasks and jobs involved. Therefore, I would argue that there is no such thing as an effective leader in all situations. What we have to do is to identify particular abilities that people have and their work preferences and match these to leadership situations.

This is in line with the view put forward by Fiedler.[1] He has argued that the important thing is to try to match the person to the job. He feels that to go the other way about and to try to change the person is very difficult and in most cases is likely to fail. Whereas a person can learn more and develop his skills and abilities, it is unlikely that he can change his personality and ways of working quite so easily. Therefore, Fiedler would argue that it is important that we try to identify a person's strengths and then enable him, through training and experience, to do a job which is in accordance with his interests.

WHAT IS THE MANAGER'S JOB?

Before we go any further, let's be clear as to some of the factors involved in managing other people. When we talk about leadership we are talking about the managing of other people's work. This is a vital part of current work in organizations. Without effective leadership, organizations will become ineffective. For a long time now the job of managing has been difficult. The old authority of the manager has begun to be undermined. Many no longer have respect for people "in authority." People have to earn the respect through their performance on the job. Just having a managerial position no longer guarantees that your word will be carried out and your orders obeyed. Today we are in the age of management by consent. Therefore, it is equally important that we begin to understand the way in which people fit into jobs and to enable them to work on tasks where their interests and abilities can apply.

The key thing about managerial work is that it does differ between various tasks as indicated above. However, the one thing which is relatively constant is the amount of time that managers will spend with other people. Stewart[2] found through her research that managers spend on average some 75 percent of their working week talking with other people. This is done in a variety of situations such as committees, interviews, informal gatherings, lunches, conferences, and many other ad hoc meetings which occur from time to time. Clearly, therefore, verbal skill is a very important aspect of managerial behavior. Managers need to be able to listen and to talk. It has often been said that managers need the "gift of gab." They also need the ability to listen and to build upon what has been said.

Managers, therefore, spend an enormous time in meetings. I have included an exercise which will help you assess how effective your meetings are. With a bit of good planning you could save hours by having your meetings better organized.

Mintzberg[3] studied five managers, all of whom were at a senior level. He noticed that although they were supposed to plan, organize, motivate, and control, their actual day-to-day work was very different. Most of their day was taken up in very short meetings, and few managers had much time to themselves. The average amount of time that any one of them had uninterrupted was ten minutes. Mintzberg drew up a list of the major jobs which he saw that managers had to perform. We shall examine these in one of the exercises in the book. You shall also have the chance to assess how you spend your work time and identify where the work pressures and opportunities come from.

WHERE ARE YOU GOING?

Besides looking at your job and your work preferences, there are a number of exercises which help you assess the next steps you can take in your career. There is a chapter looking at the things that research has shown influence people's motivation at work. Knowing the forces that are important for yourself, it is easier to identify the sort of work you should be doing.

Alongside this there is a chance to assess what sort of an organization you work in. Is it what you want? If not, do you change your job or seek to change the organization? Before getting into action, it is important to diagnose your situation clearly.

In my work as a management educator, I have found few managers who assess their own life in the way they assess a business proposition. I have, therefore, included an exercise called, "Do You Work Under Pressure?" which provides an opportunity to assess what the job does for or to you. High-pressure jobs can cause a variety of illnesses. So can low-pressure jobs where you don't have much exercise. Have a look at Chapter 8—it could help you plan your life as seriously as you plan your business deals.

Managerial work is about leadership. Some of us prefer to work as executives within an established organization. However, many managers if they had the capital would like to become entrepreneurs and run their own business. I have studied some of the key characteristics of entrepreneurs. I have, therefore, produced an exercise so that you can assess yourself in comparison to other entrepreneurs. Clearly, this is a bit of fun, but interesting. No two entrepreneurs are the same, but it is valuable to see the general trend that has emerged and make your own decision.

NOW TO THE ACTION

As I have said, this is a do-it-yourself book. It is not meant to be read as if it were a novel. My advice is, take it slowly. Work on the exercises in your spare time when you can think through what they mean. A train journey is a suitable time, or perhaps when you are on holiday. I use the exercises a lot on management development programs and that provides an excellent environment for the careful creative thinking that needs to be done.

Each exercise takes about fifteen minutes to complete. However, you should then spend at least another thirty minutes and preferably over an hour considering the implications.

Do not rush the exercises. Work at them steadily. They are designed to help you think through aspects of your work and life. The aim is to start a dialogue. It is useful, therefore, if you can discuss the exercises and the data you generate with a good friend, colleague, boss, or your spouse. The important thing is that they give you the chance to talk through your ideas rather than criticize, or attack your new half thought out ideas. Look for people who help you consider your ideas and have a willingness to listen.

The success of this book depends heavily on what you, the reader, bring to it. It is a vehicle for your experience and aspirations. Those that bring nothing will take nothing away. The book demands a lot from you. Only in that way can real progress be made. Good luck.

NOTES

1. Fiedler, F., et al., *Improving Leadership Effectiveness* (New York: John Wiley, 1976).
2. Stewart, R., *Contrasts in Management* (New York: McGraw-Hill, 1976).
3. Mintzberg, H., *The Nature of Managerial Work* (New York: Harper & Row, 1973).

CHAPTER 1

What sort of job do you have?

MANAGERIAL TIME

WHEN I HAVE ASKED MANAGERS what management involves, they usually tell me it is about leading, planning, coordinating, motivating, organizing, and a lot of other grand concepts. However, when I ask them what they actually do, they are much more specific. They say they go to meetings, make budgets, answer telephones, travel, talk, and a host of other real behavior.

But having said that, I have found that they don't all spend their time in a similar way. Managers have different ways of managing. This stems largely from the difference between, say, a research manager's job and a sales manager's job.

PEOPLE AND TIME

So what do you do? Here is a description of the people you meet at work each week. How much time do you spend with each group? Put in each of the boxes the percentage of time you think you spend with those mentioned.

People and Time

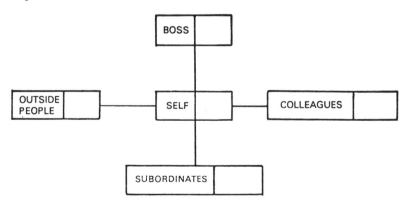

This is a quick check on how you allocate your time. Clearly to make it more accurate you need to keep a time diary. This is a difficult but useful activity. Most people do not know how they use their time at work.

Keeping a diary will enable you to see where you put most of your effort. It will also give guidance on where time can be saved.

Perhaps most important of all it will indicate to you where you should put more time and effort into work that may presently be neglected. Beyond this, such information can be valuable to you for planning your own training and development.

HOW TO MEASURE YOUR TIME

Apart from keeping a "running record" of events, whereby each minute is logged, there is a less arduous means to keep track of time.

Activity analysis: Here you identify key activities which you know from experience constitute significant parts of your job. The diary is then developed by recording the time spent on each activity. This is best done on an hourly basis so that one does not forget or estimate time allocation. An example of key activities (telephone conversations, reading, report writing, and so on) appears on page 12.

In each column the minutes spent on each activity should be recorded. These can then be totaled and percentage figures worked out for the allocation of time in particular areas.

WHAT DO WE KNOW ABOUT TIME ALLOCATION?

First and foremost, the research tells us that managers spend a lot of time talking and listening to other people. It is a key characteristic of managerial work. The average manager spends between 70 percent and 80 percent of his time in conversation at work. He does so on telephones, in corridors, in negotiations, in interviews, and at all sorts of meetings, both formal and informal.

HOURS

	1	2	3	4	5	6	7	8	Total
Telephone conversations									
Dictation									
Reading									
Report writing									
Driving/travel									
Sales meeting									
Finance meeting									
Lunch									
Selection interview									
Staff coaching, advising									
Other staff meetings									
Others									

Therefore, a key skill of a manager is his ability with words. He must be a skilled communicator. This means the ability to develop effective interpersonal relations. This point is now widely recognized, and many training programs have been developed to help managers become more skilled at interviewing, negotiating, presentations, handling grievances, and other aspects of their work demanding interpersonal skill.

The second thing we know is that managers find it very difficult to plan their time. The problem is one of interruption. The telephone rings, machines break down, or the boss wants action on a new problem. Life for the manager can be both exciting and frustrating at the same time. It has been calculated that the average period of uninterrupted time for many managers at work is about ten minutes. So as a manager you find that you have to hedge-hop from one problem to another. You have to have a good memory and be flexible to cope with the next problem or opportunity that comes your way.

Opportunity is a key word for the manager. To be successful he must find time to go beyond reacting to situations and events. He must initiate. The job of the manager will involve looking for opportunities for improvement and taking action to achieve results. The manager must, therefore, allocate time to new ideas as well as cope with the present realities.

HOW DO YOU DEFINE MANAGERIAL WORK?

Is the research manager's job the same as the sales manager's job? Clearly, they are different. But they are both managing. They manage people and allocate work. They manage assets and have to control costs. They both have to manage themselves and their time. However, there are many differences between their work. The technical aspects will of course be different. It is probable that the sort of people they meet will also differ. Certainly, their time perspective in terms of getting results will vary widely.

So how do we define the managerial job? The common component is that the manager is an *organizer*. Beyond this, it is likely that definitions will differ with the nature of the job. However, it is useful to look at the work of Henry Mintzberg,[1] who studied in detail the work of senior managers. He concluded that there were nine major *roles* that these managers had to play in the course of their jobs. I have added a tenth, which emphasizes the personal aspect of management.

It is useful to examine these managerial roles and see how far your job demands the skills involved. The roles listed on the following pages are a good basis to identify your own areas for action and where you feel the need to further extend your skill. To identify these aspects of your job, please mark the appropriate places, using this scale:

Level of Importance	*Development Required*
A = Very important to my job	3 = Need to develop my ability to perform this role
B = A normal part of my job	2 = Experienced at playing this role but need to keep up to date with current approaches
C = A minor part of my job	1 = No need to spend more time at present to further develop my ability to play this role.

To what extent does my job demand that I take on the following roles?

	Level of importance	*Development required*
1. *Figurehead* = ceremonial duties such as giving awards or public speaking and representing organization at civic occasions	_____	_____
2. *Group Leader* = being the person accountable for managing a group of people to resolve problems and agree on lines of action	_____	_____
3. *Liaison* = making contact with other groups on behalf of your own group to resolve problems and get work done	_____	_____
4. *Information* = acquisition and dissemination of information both in own group and throughout the organization	_____	_____

	Level of importance	Development required

5. *Spokesman* = representing the organization to the "outside world" in proclaiming its message through sales, public relations, or similar activities _____   _____

6. *Entrepreneur* = engaging in activity to develop new ideas, innovate, and make changes that are designed to develop the organization from its present operation to a new form _____   _____

7. *Resource Allocator* = deciding who gets what work, rewards, budgets, and other resources _____   _____

8. *Disturbance Handler* = responding to, withstanding, and coping with unexpected changes, conflicts, and pressures in the work situation _____   _____

9. *Negotiator* = bargaining as an integral part of getting the job done, whether it be with staff, colleagues, or people outside the organization _____   _____

10. *Personal* = being by oneself to think, write, compute, plan, or do other work which demands individual managerial skill _____   _____

DEVELOPING MANAGERIAL ROLES AND SKILLS

The list of roles will enable you to chart where most of your effort and energy goes. However, is that the sort of profile you want to have during the next year, or the years thereafter?

1. During the next year I should spend less time in:

_____

_____

2. During the next year I should spend more time doing:

_____

_____

_____

3. Over the next two or three months the key things I plan to achieve are:

_____

_____

_____

Actually writing down what you do is a way of clarifying things which are extremely difficult to grab hold of. The higher one goes in an organization, the more difficult it is to be precise over what one should be doing. The danger is that one ends up reacting to events rather than initiating action.

The job of the manager is to organize himself first and others second. Self-organization means knowing how you spend your time and designing a role which is relevant both to the tasks at hand and to one's own personal abilities. Throughout this book there will be a number of opportunities to look at these issues.

However, for the time being it is interesting to note that Stewart[2] has indicated that managers must concentrate upon the following three factors in deciding how to organize their work.

What are the major *demands* upon your time?

_____

_____

_____

What are the major *constraints* that you need to deal with to make improvements?

_____

_____

_____

_____

What are the major *choices* that you have in terms of developing your role?

_____

_____

_____

_____

I believe these are useful questions, in that they provide a context within which we can assess what we are doing. Each day we are thrown into meetings, have to answer telephones, respond to pieces of paper, and spend a lot of time in discussion. Where is it all leading to? It is important to have some role objectives. The higher one goes, the more difficult it is to be precise about these. Over the last few years there has been considerable interest in various techniques under the title of management by objectives (MBO) to help people clarify their work. However, on too many occasions these techniques have been seen as more paperwork and rather restrictive inspectorial devices.

More recently, we have moved toward the concept of performance appraisal. This involves a regular discussion between the manager and his subordinate to review the work that has been done and consider how it can be improved. Again this has been derided in some quarters and is yet another artificial way of managing. I believe that performance appraisal can work, provided it is done through skilled coaching. I have suggested elsewhere[3] that what we need is a constructive approach to appraisal. This will help managers at all levels gain a clearer idea of their jobs.

A Constructive Approach to Appraisal and Role Clarification

If you are going to have a discussion with your subordinates to review their performance and role with a view to improvement, I would suggest the following guidelines.

1. Let the subordinate know that this is not an individual appraisal but part of an overall policy which will involve everyone.
2. Invite the person to write down the major things he has done during the period under review—preferably three to six months and at most a year. (Beyond this the memory fades.)
3. Set a date and a time when you can meet *without being interrupted* for at least one hour.
4. At the meeting ask the subordinate to talk through the issues which he has written about. (It is preferable, if he is willing, to have this note before you meet.) However, it is important that he initiates the conversation with perhaps a starting open question from yourself, such as "How do you see your work over the last six months?"
5. For the first part of the review, concentrate upon the positive things and reinforce these by planning how they could be further developed.
6. If there are areas of weakness or inadequacy, then these should be raised later in the meeting, again in an open-ended way. Questions such as "Given your results on Product X, which have not been as good as the others, how would you see things being improved?" If the subordinate denies that things are not so good, then you need to exchange *evidence.*
7. Where the subordinate is short of ideas on improvement, then the superior should indicate his own preferences. In particular, the superior should be absolutely clear right from the beginning as to what the overall targets for the group as a whole are and ask the subordinate how he can contribute to those, as well as indicating ideas yourself.

8. Once the discussion has gone over all the issues, the superior should then agree to write up the appraisal of the subordinate and show it to him. The subordinate should have the right to add on any further points should there be any disagreement, but these should be supplementary rather than negating the superior's summary.
9. The subordinate should write independently to the superior, indicating his aims and plans for the next period to be reviewed, and this will act in such a way as to clarify his thoughts and indicate his commitments.
10. This will then provide a basis for the next review of performance either on a semiannual or an annual basis.
11. Finally, it is vital that the manager keeps in discussion with the subordinate on the issues raised in a *coaching* capacity, wherever the subordinate requests it, or in a *guiding* capacity, whenever the superior feels that the commitments and intentions are not being followed through.

KNOWING YOUR JOB

Sometimes we talk too much and don't get very far. However, there are times when we do not talk enough. I believe that managers and subordinates do not really spend as much time as they should talking through what the managerial role means and how it should be carried out. More time spent on coaching and regular appraisals can be of tremendous benefit. The guidelines above provide a framework within which roles can be clarified and support and help provided.

At the end of the day it depends upon the attitude of those people involved. Empathy and supportiveness are the key words. If a subordinate feels he is being inspected and attacked, he will not talk freely. It is vital therefore for the superior to set the right attitude. In this he should start by asking questions of an open-ended kind and leave his judgments until such time as he knows things have gone wrong. The boss who is seen to be on top of the facts, has clear standards, and is willing to talk through the problems is usually the one who is seen to be both effective and helpful in enabling a manager to clarify and perform his role.

NOTES

1. Mintzberg, H., *The Nature of Managerial Work* (New York: Harper & Row, 1973).
2. Stewart, R., *Contrasts in Management* (New York: McGraw-Hill, 1976).
3. Margerison, C., "A Constructive Approach to Appraisal," *Personnel Management*, Vol. 8, No. 7, 1976.

CHAPTER 2

So where are you now— choice or crisis?

THE CAREER PATH

WE ARE ALL MOVING FORWARD, but where are we going? Some people set definite targets and objectives. Others are more content to take life as it comes.

The higher one goes on the managerial ladder, the more difficult it becomes just to wait upon events. There is a need to anticipate events as far as possible and make plans. For example, it's no use running a business only to find out all of a sudden you have run out of cash. By forecasting and making educated guesses, it is possible to reduce your risk. Moreover, sound budgeting can make it easier to make difficult decisions.

The same is true on a personal basis. This part of the exercise is designed to give you an opportunity to see where you are in your job. In particular, it provides a framework for you to map out your work aims for the next six months.

The word "map" is used deliberately. I believe we all have personal maps which influence our behavior. However, not all of us are really conscious of our map. We may not have put our feelings into words and pictures. This particular approach helps you see where you are now and what paths are available for the short-term future. What was your first job? Does it bear any relationship to what you do now? Well, if you have moved into managing other people, it is likely that an important change will have occurred in the nature of your work. Indeed, for many people the type of work may also have changed—if you have moved, say, from a manufacturing organization to perhaps a service organization.

Let us therefore look at the overall picture. I have drawn a graph with two major trend lines on it—the technical line and the managerial line (see top of next page). This example illustrates that as you get promoted into managerial work it usually means you spend less time directly on the technical activities. For example, when the skilled craftsman

22

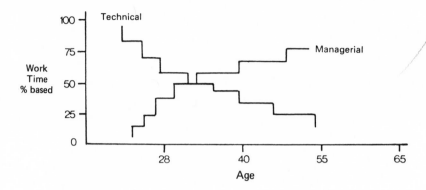

becomes a foreman, he is told explicitly not to touch the tools. This illustrates a major change in work and a shift from technical to managerial. The same is true in other work, such as when a bank clerk becomes a bank manager and so on.

List on this chart the jobs you have held so far.

Year	Age	Job Title	% Managerial Work

Now on the Work Time/Age graph below, please draw in the lines that would be most appropriate to your own career. Given your present job put a mark on the graph and estimate the time spent in direct-technical work. Then do the same for the time you spend managing other people. From this, work backward, based on the data you've listed, to show what those lines were like, say, five years ago and right back to when you started work.

Next make an estimate forward. What do you see as the changes that could occur in the next four years? Then stretch your mind to what will happen by the time you retire.

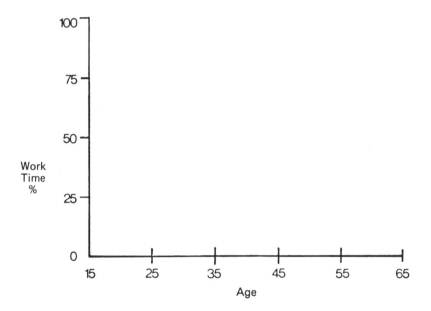

For some people, the cross-over point between technical and managerial work is a difficult move to make. One is leaving what one knows well for a more obscure future. The cross-over point can therefore be either a *choice* or a *crisis*. Some people regard it as an exciting opportunity. Others will approach it with uncertainty.

ENGINEERS AND MANAGERS—AN EXAMPLE

I was invited to conduct a study by a large organization that wanted to know "why the performance of so many of our engineers declines when they are promoted to become managers." This particular organization had over the years made a special effort to select and train engineers of the highest caliber. Senior managers could not understand, therefore, why people who had proved their technical ability should not do so well as managers.

I talked to the engineers about the change in their work. They had reached the cross-over point in their careers. Most of them felt ill-at-ease about their new work. "I seem to spend hours doing nothing except sit in meetings," said one man. "When I took over the manager's job I felt guilty that I didn't know what to do, nor did I have sufficient work to keep me occupied full time." "I had to learn how to manage my own time," said another manager.

All of the people I interviewed had moved into roles where their technical background knowledge was important, but they no longer were expected to use it in a practical way as they had before. Now they were more involved with planning, scheduling, dealing with human relations issues, and handling resource problems. They had left the job which they had qualified for and knew well, for one that was ambiguous and not easily learned.

This transition proved a difficult time for many of the engineers. The company decided, therefore, that some off-the-job training was required to help people think through their new job and get ideas on how to tackle the more open-ended aspects of their job.

WHERE ARE YOU?

Therefore, consider your own situation. Are you approaching the cross-over point, or are you presently going through it? Clearly, if you have crossed over, so to speak, this chapter can only serve to clarify the experience. However, for those approaching it or involved presently it is useful to consider what can be done.

Look at your own situation as *you* have drawn it in *Work Time/Age.*

> What does the chart tell you?
> What are the implications for action?
> What can you do now?

If you are concerned about the problems of the cross-over, there are a number of avenues you can take, and a few which have been adopted are suggested here:

☐ Discuss the issue with your boss openly, if he is willing to *coach* and help.

☐ Meet with other colleagues at the same level and hold a workshop to see what they are doing and how they are dealing with the new job.

☐ See the training manager and ask for a special course to be set up or for you to be given a chance to go to a course outside the organization.

☐ Prepare a personal action plan, such as reading, and schedule visits to other organizations to give you a wider picture of your role.

☐ Outline your concern to your subordinates in a problem-solving way and involve them in your plans.

This gives us perspective on a key time of transition in one's career. Going up the managerial ladder is not an easy task. It requires personal management.

Not every career, however, has to sacrifice the technical for the managerial. A surgeon can reach the top of his profession and still continue to practice his technical work. Yet in most organizations advancement is usually seen as a managerial promotion, except perhaps for certain areas of research or financial work.

So how does your organization operate? Are you at a point on the chart that you feel is appropriate for your age and experience? If not, what can and should you do about it?

Let us, therefore, now look at a shorter time perspective to see what factors influence the sort of work you do. This analysis will form the basis for considering how to build on or change the long-term trends we have just analyzed.

SHORT-TERM ROLE PLANNING

In all our jobs there are between four and eight main issues which we have to keep our attention upon. For ex-

ample, in my work in the business school I have the following main elements in my job:

Teaching

Administration
& supervision

Research &
development

Advising

Writing

Representative
& liaison work

Managerial work is hard to define, but we all know the
major areas within which we are expected to produce some
action. The expectations others have of you are a very useful
way in which to grasp the realities of your managerial work.
Managerial work involves responding to others' initiatives
or influencing others with your ideas. So with whom do you
meet to do your work, and with whom should you meet?

In this way you can assess the main elements in your job.
We shall then go on to look at the priorities of each element
and the pressures associated with each.

The preceding diagram illustrates my mixture. However,
in your own job there will be different elements. I have
therefore drawn another circle, so that you can fill in key
elements of your own job.

Priorities

In the next model please also indicate what you consider
are the elements' *priorities*. In short, add "1" to the element
you regard as most important, "2" to the one you would
regard as next most important, and so on.

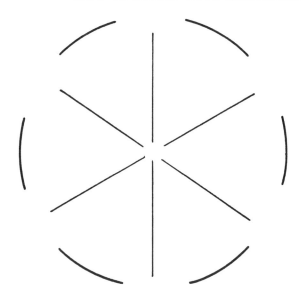

Next, indicate how much time you give to each of the elements. Place this figure in brackets next to the items that you have mentioned.

Now what is the correspondence, if any, between the priorities and the time? Are you finding that there is a close relationship or are you spending more time on things which are of less importance? How do you feel about the balance? It is often the case that we get worried because the things that demand a lot of time are not necessarily those which are important. This causes anxiety and frustration. If your priorities and time allocation are not in balance, how can you change these things?

Pressures

After identifying the priorities and the time that we give to the key elements in our job, it is also important to look at the pressures that are upon us. Add to the circle chart where the main pressures come from for each of the elements that you have described. To do this draw a line out from each of the elements. On this line write the names of people who you know have expectations of you in each of these areas. The fact that these people have expectations will invariably mean that they are exercising some pressure on you. They will want material from you. They will want you to attend meetings. They will want you to supply money. They will want you to prepare reports and a variety of other products. These are all pressures. The pressures they exercise are in terms of your doing things within a particular time and at a particular cost.

Now which of these pressures and expectations are the most difficult? If you find that some are more difficult than others, identify why this should be. How often do you meet the people in question? Is it difficult to identify what their objectives are?

EXPECTATIONS PLANNING

It is here that action plans can be developed for coping with the pressures. What needs to be done is to take a time period, say three months, and decide what you feel should be done. This will invariably mean talking to people who are also involved in the same work you are doing. You should set out what you feel is the current situation and facilitate a discussion about the work that you feel needs to be done and the support if any that you need. In talking through the situation with these people, you will invariably find that the *expectations and pressures* will become clarified, and in many cases an opportunity to resolve the difficulties will emerge. This enables you to deal with some of the ambiguity which is associated with going up the managerial ladder.

Essentially, managerial work involves getting together with other people to decide what needs to be done. It is only through arranging meetings and talking things through that the pressures and expectations can be dealt with. One of the major difficulties in crossing the managerial career ladder is that the pressures and expectations are there but are not clearly drawn.

In this next exercise, what we've attempted to do is identify the problems of priority and expectations and show a way in which these can be discussed and worked through. The idea is not radical. Indeed, it is common sense, but it does provide a practical approach to dealing with problems which are often obscure and ambiguous.

Priority issues	Whom do I talk to?	My expectations for action	Others' expectations for action
1.			
2.			
3.			
4.			
5.			
6.			
7.			
8.			
9.			
10.			
11.			
12.			
13.			
14.			
15.			

This will help crystallize the issues for discussion and the people who should be involved. However, it is equally important to try to identify what you wish to see happening on each of these and other issues over the next six to twelve months. Therefore, when you have finished this exercise, fill in your targets and objectives.

Issues	Key dates and objectives for which to aim
(a)	
(b)	
(c)	
(d)	

SUMMARY

Most managers spend a lot of time making out business plans. The same principles apply to the business of managing yourself. The exercises in this chapter provide ways of thinking about the way your career is developing. Is it haphazard or has it got some overall plan to it? By looking at the key areas of your job, you can see the priorities, the pressures, and how you are managing these. In this way it is possible to begin managing yourself as well as other people.

This is particularly important when you are crossing the line between technical and managerial work, often a time of strain due to the ambiguity associated with the new job. As one manager said to me, "I pretended to work even though I felt I had little to do. I felt rather guilty about it." Here is a clear case where expectations needed clarifying. That can only be done through discussion. As we go higher in managerial levels, the ability to "make something out of nothing" becomes more important. Analyzing your job in a positive way with others is a good first step.

CHAPTER 3

How do you prefer to work?

WE ARE LOOKING FOR SOMEONE WHO HAS TACT, SENSITIVITY, AND EMPATHY

LOOK NO FURTHER, I'M YOUR MAN! I CAN TURN ON THE TACT EASILY. AND I'VE DONE A SPECIAL COURSE IN SENSITIVITY... BUT WHAT DOES EMPATHY MEAN?

MANAGERIAL CHOICES

Do YOU KNOW your basic work preferences? Perhaps you have never been asked the question. However, most of us think a lot about the issues involved. You have heard people make comments like, "I wouldn't do his job for twice the pay," or, "My job is all right apart from the figure work and reports I have to fill in," or, "I enjoy my job when I'm left alone to get on with it quietly in my own way."

All these comments say something about the person's work preference. Given a choice, most people know what work they like and how they wish to do it. In this sense, work is similar, say, to football, golf, cricket, or any other game. In soccer, for example, I prefer to kick with my right foot because I am stronger with it. Likewise in playing golf I prefer certain clubs to others.

The same principle is true for most people at work. We have preferred ways of working. Some people enjoy work which requires precision and order. Others like work where they can exercise their creativity and ideas.

Now it is increasingly important that we understand our work preferences. Only in this way can we build upon our strengths and help overcome our weaker areas. The *Managerial Preference Index* provides a simple guide to work preferences. It is an introduction to an area which is expanding rapidly in terms of research knowledge.

THE MANAGERIAL PREFERENCE INDEX

Fill in the following questionnaire to indicate how you prefer to operate. Allocate a number from the scale which best corresponds with your own preference.

WHAT DO THE SCORES MEAN?

Each person has a preferred way of doing work. Some of us like to be very methodical. Others prefer to be more op-

0	1	2	3
Does not describe my preferred approach at all	Describes my preferred approach only a little	Describes my preferred approach a fair amount of the time	Describes my preferred approach most of the time

	C Column	*E Column*
Systematically	_____	
Creatively		_____
With hard facts	_____	
Inventing/designing		_____
Building/producing	_____	
Theorizing		_____
Using imagination		_____
In orderly way	_____	
Planning	_____	
Exploring possibilities		_____
Spontaneous action		_____
Searching and changing		_____
Consolidating	_____	
Taking risks		_____
Using insight		_____
Being practical	_____	
Using intuition		_____
Rationally	_____	
Methodically	_____	
With change and newness	_____	_____
With standards and systems	_____	
With real things	_____	
Total:	_____	_____
Analysis Total:	Total = ____ × 10 / 3	Total = ____ × 10 / 3
Percentage Total:	_____	_____

erational and to do what seems appropriate at the time. The *Managerial Preference Index* examines these two approaches.

The *C Column* stands for the *Controlling Approach*. A high score here indicates that you prefer to gather information in an orderly way. You like to work with facts and to plan carefully the work you do. If possible, you prefer working to rules and guidelines or setting them up if they don't already exist.

A high score on the controlling approach indicates a preference for a clear approach to problems. Efforts, therefore, will be directed toward establishing order, following through a plan, and working in a methodical way.

People with a high C score often have high standards for the work they do and expect others to keep to them. These standards can be technical ones or based on personal beliefs. For some, this leads to a decisive, judgmental style. For others, it means a supportive, helping approach to establishing order.

A high score does not mean you will actually behave in such a way. It indicates only your preferences. Your job may not allow a highly methodical approach. However, it is likely you will develop an interest or hobby that enables you to fulfill your preferences.

The *E Column* stands for the *Explorer's Approach*. A high E score indicates that you prefer to gather information in an innovative but not particularly systematic way. The preference is to follow the task at hand and gather what information seems to you to be of interest and relevance at the time. The E approach is therefore more intuitive, more spontaneous, and more open than the methodical approach.

A high E score will, therefore, indicate that you prefer to use your imagination, consider a range of possibilities, theorize, search for new ways of doing things, and work in an innovative way. There is a strong likelihood that you will enjoy designing and an inventive kind of work, where you can be creative. Moreover, the person with a high E score is likely to have leaps of insight which go beyond the facts immediately available. High E scorers enjoy searching out new ways—some do it in a practical way, others in a more theoretical way.

HOW TO SEE YOUR PROFILE

The chart below enables you to draw your profile as indicated in the index that you completed. It is likely that each person has one dominant work preference approach. The chart is a basis for comparing profiles. Some people find it difficult to work together but cannot understand why this is so. It is often useful to compare work preference profiles and discuss how each person does his job. The discussion can lead to understanding the other person's preferences and skills, so that you both complement each other's work more than previously. It may also lead to some work rearrangement to make use of people's particular skills and preferences.

If you have one particular dominant preference, it is useful to spend some time developing the other area. The higher one goes in management, the more important it is that one is able to be both methodical and operationally creative. Therefore, if you are strong on one and not the

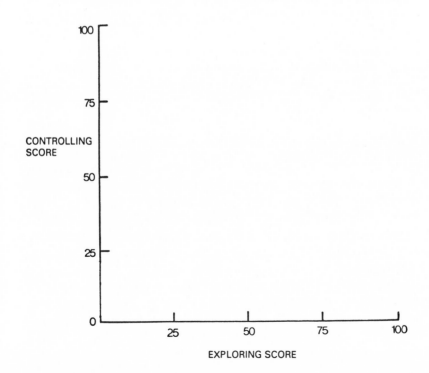

other, take time out to develop skills in the other area, even though it may be against your natural preference.

HOW IMPORTANT ARE THESE IDEAS?

Job Choice

Considerable work has been done by occupational psychologists to identify why people choose their particular jobs. The evidence shows that job choice is not a random activity. Most people have a set of personal interests which push toward or away from given jobs.

So look at your own job. Is it the one you chose when you left school? How happy are you doing the job? How many times have you changed your job?

Most people search for a job that matches their interests. However, when you leave school it is difficult to make a choice because you don't know what is available. Consequently, many people take a job which is unsuitable for them because they don't really know their own interests, or because they don't know what the available jobs really mean in terms of the work required.

Therefore, it is of prime importance that the research work done in the field of work preference is applied to both recent graduates and people in mid-career making job decisions.

Choosing Staff

If you are in a position where you select staff it is vital that you know something about people's work preferences and how they relate to the job you are offering. The usual way to discover such information is to conduct an interview and examine a person's background. These may not, however, tell you if the candidate's preferred way of working is appropriate.

Increasingly, personality and work preference tests are being used. Managers need to know what a test can and can't do and how to use the data. If you spend a lot of time selecting staff, then the best advice is to have an in-depth course on the techniques available, where you experience them for yourself.

Building an Effective Team

The task of a manager is to bring people together to do a job that could not be done as effectively or efficiently by one man working alone. It is important, therefore, to have in any team a balance of talents. Just as in a soccer team you don't want too many goalkeepers or strikers, then in a work team you need to balance the work preferences.

This is more than a matter of selection. It means bringing people together in such a way that they complement each other.

Now because there will be different work preferences, the manager needs to spend time helping the person who wants specific details to understand the innovative, intuitive sales type and vice versa. I believe the manager can only do this if he has a sound understanding of individual differences and the work preferences of such people.

Training

Work preferences tell us a lot about the things in which we will or will not invest energy. As a result we are likely to become more skilled at particular tasks but to overlook others. A manager who is aware of his work preferences will guard against ignoring the things he does not like doing.

This is particularly important when it comes to training oneself and others. To take the soccer analogy there is a danger that one will only practice shooting with, say, one's right foot if that is where your strength is. To improve, one must also practice with the left foot. So it is in work situations. The training needs to cover both strong and weak preferences.

LEADERSHIP PREFERENCES

The work I have conducted with my colleague Ralph Lewis suggests that the work preferences people have strongly influence not only the job they choose but the way they go about their tasks, and also the way they are likely to behave in leadership situations.

The following model illustrates some of the key ideas to emerge from this work and identifies some different ways in which people prefer to work.

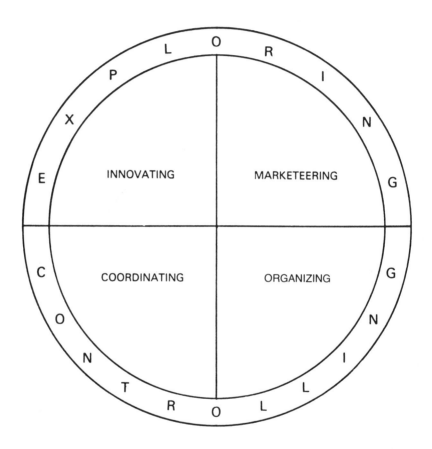

The key point is that we all behave in each area mentioned above, but we like to operate in one more than in others. As we have already shown in the *Managerial Preference Index,* there is a tendency for people to prefer either an exploring or a controlling approach to work situations. Let us look at this in more detail.

Marketeering

Thus, an example of the *marketeer* is the person who gets a good idea and takes great risks to make the idea a success. Often such people set up in business. If they are good at judging risk and establishing some discipline over their ideas, then they can and do make a lot of money. Marketeers are not all business entrepreneurs, however. They typically enjoy having an adventurous life and putting ideas into practice. They hate routine and search for excitement. In this sense they are in the marketplace and love to trade, whether it be in business or in social life, where they present themselves in an attractive and often aggressive way to get their ideas into action. They emphasize exploring in a practical way.

Innovating

The innovator is also an explorer but is less inclined to take high practical risks. The innovator will dream up new ideas, create great works of art, or develop new ways of doing things. He will more often than not leave it to others to organize his ideas. His main interest lies in chasing possibilities. He enjoys creative work where he can exercise his curiosity. Innovators dislike routine and can be unpredictable insofar as they wish to solve a problem or work in their own way.

Coordinating

The coordinator emphasizes standards, values, and principles. In essence he likes to have an organized mind. He will spend time trying to convince others that standards and principles are important and possibly be oriented to people rather than things. He likes order but works at a conceptual level rather than directly with things. He is, therefore, concerned with controlling ideas and establishing clarity. Such a person can be very perceptive and can help others to resolve (control) differences of opinion. In this sense, he helps bring order by helping people to gather all the facts and to agree on principles. At its best this behavior enables others to develop and agree upon plans, which previously have been innovative ideas subject to great argument between people holding strong judgments. In this sense, the coordinator can be a catalyst helping to create order from conflict.

Organizing

In contrast, the other main controlling type is the person who prefers to operate systems, and to maintain practical order of machines, money, and other tangible items. Such a person again will emphasize the importance of working with facts and be good at dealing with details. This type of person, however, concentrates on making things happen. He is unhappy just thinking about things. The name of his game is providing an organization structure where he and others can do things. He is, therefore, likely to get involved with or lead a group of people doing a work task, rather than talking about it or planning it.

WHAT RANGE DO YOU HAVE?

Now in real life all of us can operate in these ways. However, given a choice we usually prefer one area more than another. Therefore, we look for jobs and opportunities that will permit us to behave in accord with our major preference.

Each organization needs a good balance of each group of people. In particular, we need people who are flexible and can cover a wide area of the circle outlined earlier.

From such an approach you can begin to develop a map of how you see yourself and others. Does the pattern show any marked drift to the marketeer, the innovator, the coordinator, or the organizer quadrant? How well balanced is the coverage for each area? Does the profile seem appropriate for the type of job you have? What changes if any do you wish to make either in your job or in your managerial work profile?

Now what changes do you feel you should aim to make in the next twelve months? To conclude this chapter there is, therefore, a self-completion section, where you can identify the points you wish to develop.

Exploring: In my job the key things that I am accountable for exploring are:

_____

_____

_____

_____

Controlling: In my job the key things that I am accountable for controlling are:

_____

_____

_____

_____

Issues for Action

Marketeering: I intend to

_____

_____

_____

_____

Organizing: I intend to

_____

_____

_____

_____

Innovating: I intend to

_____

_____

_____

_____

Coordinating: I intend to

_____

_____

_____

_____

Now assess the members of your staff team on the points raised in this chapter. Do you have too many explorers or not enough controllers? It is the team balance and staff mix that is important. Therefore, in concluding this section note down the people in your team and summarize your view of their contribution.

Member's Name	Main Strengths	Areas for Improvement

Given the demands of the jobs these people do, is the team well balanced? If not, you clearly need to try to develop these individuals in the areas mentioned or select new people to cover the weak areas.

REFERENCES

Bischof, L. *Interpreting Personality Theories.* New York: Harper & Row, 1970.

Eysenck, H., and Wilson, G. *Know Your Own Personality*. New York: Penguin, 1976.

Holland, J. *Making Vocational Choices*. Englewood Cliffs, N.J.: Prentice-Hall, 1973.

Jung, C. G. *Psychological Types*. London: Routledge, 1923.

Margerison, C., Lewis, R., and Hibbert, C. "Training Implications of Work Preferences." *Journal of European Industrial Training*. Vol. 2, No. 3, 1978.

CHAPTER 4

How do you see yourself?

IMAGES OF SELF

WE ALL HAVE A SELF-IMAGE. A self-image is a mental picture of how we see ourselves. It is this self-picture that is so important in guiding our everyday behavior.

If we see ourselves as able, intelligent, resourceful, and knowledgeable, it is likely we will behave differently from those who see themselves as anxious, unsure, slow, and inadequate. It might be hard to admit such feelings, but they invariably reflect themselves in our behavior.

Our self-image, or self-concept, is therefore fundamental to the sort of life we lead. It reflects not only who we are but it indicates our aspirations.

Here you have an opportunity to identify a number of characteristics of your own self-picture. This index will only deal with particular preferences of yourself in the context of work. The index does *not* try to paint a total picture of you. No index can do that. All people differ in their preferences from time to time and in different situations.

So it is preferences we are assessing. We are not, repeat *not*, measuring personality. The value of this index lies in the way you use it. Ideas on how this can be done are given after the index.

PERSONAL PREFERENCE INDEX: HOW I WOULD DESCRIBE MYSELF AT WORK

Each of the columns in the next exercise provides an insight into different aspects of your self-picture when at work.

Column S = Sociability Score

This gives an indication of how you perceive yourself in your relationships with others at work. Some people prefer to be seen as friendly and as people who enjoy the company of others. Such people will therefore seek out others for

48

conversation and be open to receiving other people and their ideas.

A high sociability score only indicates you prefer to interact with other people. It says nothing about how effective you are at work or in interpersonal relations. A high sociability score therefore indicates your intentions and preferences.

A low sociability score indicates you probably prefer to work more with machines, objects, or systems. Such a score indicates that you prefer working in an environment where you can have more time to yourself rather than having to regularly make conversation with others.

Column P = Power Score

This gives an indication of your preference for having a job in which you can exercise some control over proceedings. Some people prefer work where they can influence organizational decisions. There are other people who have little interest in exercising such power.

A high power score indicates that you are interested in obtaining, or maintaining, a position where you can have control of resources and people to get work done. Again, a high score does not say how effective you are in the use of such power if you possess it. The score serves to give an indication of your interests.

To get a more realistic indication of what power means, think about your own organization. How much power over decisions do you have compared to the person in the next department? Who has power over you in the organization in terms of work allocation, budgets, promotions, and salary increases? What position in the organization would you like to have next, and how much organizational control will it give you?

A low power score means of course that you exhibit little interest in controlling the issues mentioned above. Your interests in the organization will lie in other areas. For example, people in research frequently say that their main interest is in doing scientific investigations rather than making decisions on the way the organization will work. Such a person can work extremely hard but have little interest in obtaining organizational power.

Column A = Achievement Score

This gives an indication of your need for achievement within your present organization. The scores you gave reflect the extent to which you see yourself pushing onward and outward to given targets. Some people have a clear idea of their targets. Others are keen to succeed but are not sure at what. Both are people who will see themselves as high achievers. It is likely they will live out their self-image by working hard to make things happen.

A high achievement score therefore only says what you perceive to be your approach to work. It says nothing about what you will actually do in real life. A person with a high achievement score has a self-picture of one who sets high targets, wants to succeed, and is prepared to work hard. The person who is actually successful translates these attitudes into a workable plan, follows a particular path to the goals set, and organizes his life so as to achieve the targets. You can, therefore, ask yourself to what extent you convert your intentions into workable plans for achievement.

A person with a low score on preferred achievement is indicating that his interests lie elsewhere. A low score usually means that such a person does not prefer to work in a highly competitive, stressful, probably risky situation. He therefore opts for a different pattern of work. In this he can be as conscientious, loyal, hard-working, and persevering as others, but will not work to the limit of his capacity.

To complete this index please allocate a *score* for each item in the following columns based on the scale below:

0	1	2	3
Does not describe me	Describes me occasionally	Describes me a fair amount	Describes me quite a lot

	S	P	A
Warm	_____		
Deliberate		_____	
Inventive			_____

	S	P	A
Thorough			___
Confident		___	
Foresight			___
Sympathetic	___		
Single-minded		___	
Generous	___		
Sets targets			___
Recognition important		___	
Enthusiastic			___
Strong-willed		___	
Responsible		___	
Empathic	___		
Ambitious		___	
Industrious			___
Optimistic			___
Conscientious	___		
Open	___		
Likes position of authority		___	
Opportunity-minded			___
Time-conscious			___
Friendly	___		
Persistent			___
Control important		___	
Conversationalist	___		
Idealistic		___	
Affable and friendly	___		
Totals:	___	___	___
Analysis Total:	Total =	Total =	Total =
	$\times$ 10	$\times$ 10	$\times$ 10
	3	3	3
Percentage Score:	___	___	___

HOW IMPORTANT ARE SOCIABILITY, POWER, AND ACHIEVEMENT?

1. *Sociability:* How important is it for the boss to be sociable? Well, if he wants his staff to have a positive attitude toward work, then he needs to take account of his relationships. But that does *not* mean the boss has to be easygoing, regarded as a personal friend, or a hail-fellow-well-met type.

The boss requires the ability to have empathy with his staff. This involves being prepared to listen to problems, to inform them of issues, and to involve people in decision making when it affects them. The boss, therefore, is expected to have the interests of his staff at heart, but not necessarily to be friendly.

He is the sort of person whom staff feel able to talk to as an equal without actually being equal. The boss, therefore, has to indicate the relationship he wishes to develop. It is a delicate balance between being overfriendly and familiar and being distant and detached.

In general, the extrovert is in danger of becoming too sociable, while the introvert is likely to become too detached. There is a middle ground. It is the boss's job to find what is required.

2. *Power:* The powerful person in an organization is able to influence people and resources. To a large extent, though, power is a subjective thing. Other people attribute power to others, insofar as they agree or go along with what is being proposed. The really powerful person, of course, has sanctions to impose on those who don't agree with his position. Therefore, today most managers have far less power than their predecessors.

We know from research that some people enjoy using power and will seek out positions (or create them if they don't exist) whereby they can exercise power over situations and people. The evolution of modern organizations has reduced the unilateral power of the top manager. Today, committees, working parties, unions, works councils, and other structural features mean that top managers have to consider others far more in their decision making.

The important thing about power is the way it is used. Subordinates will tend to judge the boss by a standard of fairness. Anyone who has power and authority over others has to decide what is fair and reasonable. "Who should be promoted, what allocation of work should be made, how are grievances dealt with?" These are all questions which bring out the way power is used. If subordinates feel they have had a fair hearing, that the boss acted fairly, then there will be little conflict. However, where people feel that power and authority are being used to undermine them or belittle them, then they will usually resist.

Power is, therefore, a crucial factor in leadership. It is hard to define at the personal level. However, we spend a lot of time in defining jobs and the authority that people have in those jobs. Once they leave that job they leave behind their authority. Nevertheless, people carry with them their own personal style and personal power of influence.

It is, therefore, interesting to see what McClelland and Burnham[1] have said which I believe summarizes some of the important research on this subject.

> The manager's job seems to call more for someone who can influence people than for someone who does things better on his own. In motivational terms, then, we might expect the successful manager to have a greater "need for power" than need to achieve.

The main point, however, is that people who have power must be seen to use it in a reasonable way. McClelland, therefore, has written:

> The general conclusion of these studies is that the top manager of a company must possess a high need for power, that is, a concern for influencing people. However, this need must be disciplined and controlled so that it is directed toward the benefit of the institution as a whole and not toward the manager's personal aggrandizement. Moreover, the top manager's need for power ought to be greater than his need for being liked by people.

Leaders who were seen to use power well did so while maintaining relationships with people. This is a delicate balance. In short, McClelland argues that such people have a high need for power, a low need for sociability, but a high degree of inhibition in terms of their concern for maintaining a sound organization and achieving the task within disciplined plans, budgets, and schedules. This is one of the most interesting paradoxes of the controlled use of power that we need to understand in developing our own leadership style.

Power and authority are a key aspect of the leadership process. Anyone who has control over jobs, rewards, work, and appointments to decision-making bodies has power. However, he is only going to get commitment and followership if he is seen to be fair in his use of that power.

Now think of your own organization. Can you remember a time when a manager exercised power inappropriately? What did he do and what happened as a result? What was the feeling of the people involved?

Similarly, think of a time when the person has exercised power in a way people felt to be fair and reasonable. What happened and how was the matter handled?

In considering such instances, we can learn a lot about the proper use of power. It is important that we do so in our modern organizations, where problem-solving skills will have to replace unilateral power and authority.

3. *Achievement:* A lot of research has gone into the achievement motive, as Professor David McClelland[2] has called it. He argues that the achievement (together with the power) motive are the most important for business people. His studies show that national prosperity seems to be linked to the need for achievement of the people in a country. Moreover, their need for achievement, he believes, is inculcated early in childhood through the stories they are told.

Business people are usually high achievers. That is, they set standards and work hard to reach them. However, studies of successful managers show they know how to set realistic targets. Typically, the successful manager is one who sets a target for himself and his group which is reachable but with effort. That is, he does not set targets which are too easy. Likewise, he does not set targets which are out of sight. Instead, he assesses the situation and plans to reach a target that is hard enough to be a challenge, but not so far away as to be unrealistic.

McClelland believes it is possible to train people to set realistic targets and, therefore, to improve achievement. Clearly, the management-by-objectives schemes were an integral part of this thinking, but often backfired when they were seen as inspectorial and checking devices. We have now moved toward a concept of appraisal and self-development which should enable people to decide more clearly for themselves what they wish to obtain.

Alongside this will develop the practice of setting objectives and targets on a group basis. This has been called management by group objectives. If done well, it is a powerful form of raising the level of achievement. People typically do not like to let their group down. Therefore, once group objectives have been agreed on, there is personal pride at stake for each individual in making sure his part of the work is completed satisfactorily.

This group approach to objective setting is increasingly reflected in tasks such as the budgeting process. Rather than budgets being passed down to subordinates as standards to be met, a new process of collective budget setting is developing. Here each staff member works out what he feels is reasonable for his area, and this is fed into the meeting with budgets prepared by other colleagues. Out of the subsequent discussion comes a total budget with agreed area or local targets which have been agreed to on a participative basis. This can have a marked effect on the motivation of staff to achieve the targets insofar as they have prepared and talked through their own ideas in relation to others. At the end of the day, it is this determination to achieve which makes the difference as to whether the targets are met.

WHAT ACTION CAN YOU TAKE?

Sociability: Should you wish to learn more about relationships, then take one of the many courses on interpersonal skills. These exist at all business schools or large consulting organizations and are often described as leadership, managing people at work, motivation, or communication courses.

Beyond this, identify the particular skills you wish to develop such as interviewing, public speaking, feeling at ease over business lunches, or interviewing staff, and then try out new ideas gradually. For example, don't try to become an extrovert if you are basically an introvert. However, you can try to develop your relationships by asking open-ended questions (such as, "How do you feel about. . . ?"). This will start discussions, provided people feel you are genuinely interested in what they say. Also try joining your staff at a tea break or lunch from time to time. Being sociable in itself will not produce better managerial results. It is the extent to which your behavior is relevant and appropriate to your staff that counts.

Power: The short answer is get promoted if you want to increase your power. But how do you get promoted? Clearly, qualifications may help, but performance on your present job is probably the main thing. However, why do you want power? Do you wish to reform the company, exploit people, get your own way, or make sure that the organization develops properly? There are many reasons why people want power. By answering the "why" question, it is likely you will get a clearer idea of what action to take.

Achievement: Well, if you wish to produce more, find out what is holding you back. Is it lack of knowledge, technique, technology, or resource? Look to the blockages in the organization. In that sense, the problem may be easily overcome. The physical constraints to achievement are usually easier to deal with than personal issues.

High-achieving people usually believe they can achieve things. They have an inner confidence, a range of ideas, a resource that pushes them onward. Do you have an inner drive or do you have to be pushed? Eric Berne[3] has said we are all given scripts by our parents that tell us what we can and cannot do. These he calls our "permissions." Do you have permission to achieve? If not, who said you couldn't? Cast aside such limitations. Achievement is largely a matter of believing, so start by having a bit more faith in yourself and follow this up with determination to succeed.

HOW DO YOUR FRIENDS AND COLLEAGUES COMPARE?

If you think these three concepts are important, think about people you know who perform well on one or more. What do they do that you feel is appropriate? Models are important as a basis for our learning. In that sense, we all learn from each other. So what do those people do who are good managers and exemplify the appropriate level of sociability, power, and achievement? Maybe this is where our learning and development should start.

In particular, look at such people and yourself, comparing their profiles also on the explorer and controller dimensions mentioned in the previous chapter.

NOTES

1. McClelland, D.C., and Burnham, D., "Power Is the Great Motivator," *Harvard Business Review,* March 1976.
2. McClelland, D.C., "That Urge to Achieve," *Organizational Psychology,* edited by D. Kolb et al. (Englewood Cliffs, N.J.: Prentice-Hall, 1970).
3. Berne, Eric, *What Do You Say After You Say Hello?* (New York: Grove, 1972).

REFERENCES

McClelland, D.C. *The Achieving Society.* New York: Van Nostrand Reinhold, 1961.
—*Motivating Economic Achievement.* New York: Free Press, 1967.
—*Power, the Inner Experience.* New York: Irvington Publishers, 1975.

CHAPTER 5

What motivates you and others?

FORCES OF INFLUENCE

MOTIVATION HAS BECOME something of a vogue word in management. A great deal of study has been conducted to identify the factors that influence people to behave in particular ways. I suspect that a lot of the interest in motivation is often manipulative. That is, people like to know what motivates others, so conditions can be arranged to switch on or switch off the motivational button.

Our purpose here is very different. Instead of asking how we can get someone else to do what we want, we shall consider what we want to do and how we can adopt the appropriate action. We shall, therefore, examine *our own* motivations. In particular, we shall look at the implications they have for the way we manage.

First of all, let us consider a straightfoward analysis of the forces that influence us. As shown below, these can be divided into those that are within us and those that are outside of us.

Personal Forces

These are forces essentially *within* ourselves. At the simplest level, we act when we are hungry or cold. We feel the need to overcome these conditions and act accordingly. A personal force of a different kind can be our beliefs. For example, if we hold strong religious, political, or humanistic values, these can influence our behavior in particular directions. In a similar way, when you set yourself a target, such as passing an examination or in my case writing this book, then this becomes a motivational force. It becomes a matter of personal importance. Therefore, when looking at this aspect of motivation, ask yourself, "What do I do because of personal needs?"

Push Forces

Other people, such as the family, have expectations of you and indicate how they want you to behave. In this way, they exercise a *push* influence upon you. This may or may not motivate you to act. Nevertheless, if you feel pressure from others, then this is a push force. In the work situation the expectations of your superior are usually a major push factor. Likewise, the pressures exerted on you by your subordinates and colleagues are key forces. In such situations, you can ask, "What expectations do others have of me that exert a push force upon me?"

Pull Forces

As the term implies, *pull* forces refer to those factors which exist outside of yourself and attract you. There are lots of pull forces in our consumer society. Things like new cars, new houses, holidays, and other possessions can be attractive. However, to obtain such things we usually need to work to earn the necessary money. Does work, therefore, become a pull force for you? If your work really interests you, then it is a pull force. How far do the wages pull you forward? Beyond that, what about the pull forces associated with the possibility of promotion, more pay, a bigger job, and so on? These factors are all external to yourself and pull forces if they encourage you to exert effort to achieve them.

THE FORCES

This simple analysis builds upon the major theories of motivation. For example, Kurt Lewin[1] believed that everyone had certain psychological needs that provided the initial spur to action. Hull, another psychologist, had referred to a similar factor which he called "drive." Lewin said that each person saw objects such as cars and holidays as having differing value or valences. In this case, the pull of the object had its influence because of the value assigned it by the individual.

Now this individual self-determining view of motivation differs from the theory of B.F. Skinner.[2] He rejects the idea that individual drives, needs, values, valences, and other internal states can be measured. According to Skinner, you need to look carefully at the push and pull forces. If a person responds to a pull force, whether it be money, status, gifts, or whatever, then he calls that reinforcement. In short, a person is likely to repeat behavior that is rewarded by an appropriate pull force. If he acts to avoid or reduce a push force, this is also motivating but is called a negative rather than positive reinforcement.

These theories have similarities but are fundamentally different. Look at your own motivation. Do you act mainly because of personal forces that are decided by yourself? Alternatively, do you respond and react to push and pull forces that exist outside of yourself? Well, maybe it's a bit of both. Some of us are strong-willed, self-determined, and will tread a path regardless of the external pulls, whether they be attractive or distractive. Others are more inclined to see what is on offer and respond to that which seems appropriate at the time.

WHAT LIES BETWEEN PUSH AND PULL?

In terms of work, we need to keep with the theory just a bit longer. The reason is that we need to look at what people want, what they expect, and what they think will happen. You see, motivation is as much in the mind as it is in any objective reality.

Another psychologist, Vroom,[3] has proposed an idea called "expectancy theory," which says: People will act if they expect to achieve results and the results are important to them. This has since been developed by others and can be summarized in the following questions:

1. What am I *expected* to do?
2. If I do it, is it likely I will *be able* to do the task?
3. If I achieve the task, *is it likely to be sufficiently rewarded?*
4. What *implication* does the task have for my job?
5. Will all this effort *satisfy my other needs?*

These are the questions that people often ask themselves when asked to do overtime work, take on a special job, or just extend the normal area of activity. It implies that people do see work from an exchange viewpoint. That is, they will exchange effort for reward provided they feel able and the conditions are right. In this sense, it is a pull theory. However, in reality most motivation is a function of push, pull, and personal forces.

YOUR WORK AND YOU

Now let us consider the work you do. The index below is open-ended. There are no fixed answers. You are invited to write in your own response to complete the sentences. In completing the sentences, please put the words and phrases that first come to your mind. In this way you will begin to get a spontaneous reaction and an insight into your motivation.

1. I go to work because _____

_____

_____

_____

2. Work to me means _____

_____

_____

_____

3. The best part of work is _____

_____

_____

_____

4. My job is _____

_____

_____

_____

5. Motivation to work comes from _____

_____

_____

_____

6. The worst part of my work is _____

_____

_____

_____

7. If I made one change to make my work more interesting, I would_____

_____

_____

_____

8. My motivation would improve if _____

_____

_____

_____

9. My motivation would decline if_____

_____

_____

_____

10. My ambition is to _____

_____

_____

_____

The answers to the above should give you an insight into
your current work situation. Do you feel motivated to do a
good job? Where does the motivation come from? Previ-

ously I have suggested you can be pushed, be pulled, or be internally motivated by your own requirements. Now how have you answered the sentences? Do the replies indicate that you are reasonably satisfied and motivated or relatively dissatisfied? Does your present job give you what you presently require?

Let us, therefore, look at motivation in relation to some research that has been done. Again, you can assess yourself.

YOUR WORK INDEX

How important are these factors to you in motivating you to work hard? Assign to each factor a score from the following scale:

1	2	3	4	5
Of low importance	Of little importance	Of fair importance	Of considerable importance	Of major importance

Factors	*Score*
(a) Considerate supervision	_____
(b) Job with an important purpose	_____
(c) Good pension	_____
(d) Achievement opportunities	_____
(e) High pay	_____
(f) Clear company policy	_____
(g) Recognition for good work	_____
(h) Clean working conditions	_____
(i) Advancement and promotion	_____
(j) Job security	_____
(k) Job allows participation and decision making	_____
(l) High position in organization	_____
(m) Job responsibility	_____
(n) Pleasant relationships with others	_____
(o) Job that stretches you (personal growth)	_____
(p) Freedom to organize own time and variety	_____
(q) Job with security	_____

SOME RESEARCH FINDINGS

The above index incorporates issues examined in a number of research studies. Probably the most famous is the work of Herzberg[4] and his colleagues. They have argued that two major conditions are needed for people to be motivated at work: hygiene factors and motivating factors.

The hygiene factors don't positively motivate people, but without them people will not work hard. In short, they have to be present but don't lead to increased effort from people. *The motivating factors* can influence performance, provided they are used at the appropriate time.

In this test for your job, score yourself according to the scale given for *Your Work Index*. The lettered items refer back to that list.

Hygiene Score	*Motivating Score*
(a) _____	(b) _____
(c) _____	(d) _____
(e) _____	(e) _____
(f) _____	(g) _____
(h) _____	(i) _____
(j) _____	(k) _____
(l) _____	(m) _____
(n) _____	(o) _____
(q) _____	(p) _____
Total _____	Total _____

It is assumed for this purpose that the items are related but that there are two independent scores. (It should be noted, however, that I have put "High Pay" on both Hygiene and Motivating scores, as there is considerable argument over where this factor should be placed.) The graph on the opposite page gives you a second way to check on how your job rates.

As a guide, the scores below the graph can be used as a basis for comparison with your own.

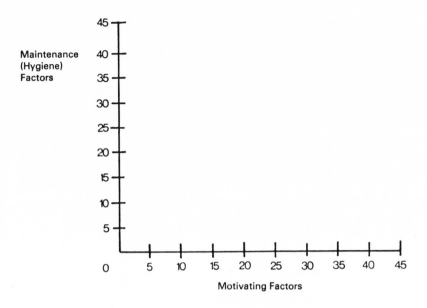

Over 35	High Score
Between 26–34	Fairly High Score
Between 16–25	Fairly Low Score
Under 15	Low Score

The Herzberg theory has been used widely by managers as the basis for redesigning a job. The term "job enrichment" has been the basis of such efforts. However, other researchers have said the two elements of hygiene and motivation are too simple. For example, perhaps different types of people require different forms of motivation. For one person, good working conditions is the most important thing, but for someone else it may be of minor importance.

Your Work Index needs to be judged in terms of your own feelings. What weight do you attach to the scores? Do they make sense given your feelings about your present job? This is the key test. All theory should be tested against personal experience.

What, therefore, are the implications for you? Are you in the right job? Do you need to change the job to fit your style or will you change your job?

Whatever you do, consider the findings of recent research,[5] which point to key factors that seem to be of importance in influencing people's motivation at work. Score again on the 5-point scale by choosing one number for each question.

1	2	3	4	5
Very little	A little	Medium	A lot	A great deal

Score

Variety	Do I want a job with a wide range of activities?	_____
Autonomy	Do I want a job where I have a major influence over plans and schedules?	_____
Task identity	Do I want a job where I complete a whole piece of work which can be seen as a product of my effort?	_____
Feedback	How important is it that I get regular information on how well I am doing?	_____
Significance	To what extent is it important that I have a job that has a real purpose and meaning for me?	_____
Relationships	How important is it to have a job where I can meet with others?	_____
Friendship	To what extent is it important that the job enables me to make and work with friends?	_____

If these things are important, as well as money, job security, and the other "hygiene" factors, then look carefully before choosing your next job. However, for the time being what do your staff want and what do they get? Can you do anything about their jobs and motivation? This matrix gives you a basis for comparing the factors influencing motivation at different levels.

Give a score based on the following scale for the jobs described. Indicate how you feel the jobs score on the factors mentioned.

1	2	3	4	5
Very little	A little	Medium	A lot	A great deal

	Two levels above yours	One level above	Your level	One level below	Two levels below
Variety					
Autonomy					
Task identity					
Feedback					
Significance					
Relationships					
Friendship					
Total					

SUMMARY

What do you want from work and to what extent does your present job enable you to obtain it? In theory, for a person to do an effective job there has to be an overlap between his work interests and his self-interests.

Now what, therefore, are the things you are looking for in your job from the factors outlined in this chapter? Is it possible to reorganize your job to help improve your motivation? If not, should you change your job so as to match your personal interests? Many people take a job early in life for which they are not suited and then find it difficult to change. The accountant and the engineer are good examples where long training serves to draw people into a job which may or may not suit their own preferences. The key point, however, is to be aware of one's interests and motivations and either adapt the job or change to another occupation.

So in concluding this section, look carefully at your own interests and motivations, your present job, and the organizational conditions.

To what extent do these factors link together to provide conditions where you are highly motivated to do your best? If they don't link together, what can you, and what will you, do?

Change your interests and motivations.

Change your job or reorganize your present job.

Change the organizational conditions.

In short, look at your own feelings about your current situation. What should you do next?

NOTES

1. Lewin, K., *Field Theory in Social Science* (London: Tavistock, 1947).
2. Skinner, B.F., *Beyond Freedom and Dignity* (New York: Alfred A. Knopf, 1971).
3. Vroom, V., *Motivation and Work* (New York: John Wiley, 1964).
4. Herzberg, F., *Work and the Nature of Man* (New York: Thomas Y. Crowell, 1966).
5. Hackman, J., Oldham, G., Janson, R., and Purdy, K., *A New Strategy for Job Enrichment,* Technical Report No. 3, Department of Administrative Sciences, Yale University, 1974.

CHAPTER 6

Are your meetings successful?

P.S. How do you know?

MEETINGS—DO THEY WORK?

"I'm sorry but Mr. Roberts is in a meeting at the moment. Can you ring back later?"

We have all had that sort of reply. There is a high probability that if you ring any manager at work he will be in a meeting. As we noted earlier, most managers spend between 70 percent and 90 percent of their time in work meetings.

Meetings are a major source of communication and are essential for sound decision making. But how successful are they?

Do you find meetings dragging on, wasting your time, and not helping you? Do you feel there are too many meetings? When you organize a meeting, how can you tell if it is using the talents of the people present?

HOW TO ASSESS BUSINESS MEETINGS

All managers spend considerable periods of time in business meetings. Rarely do we evaluate in a systematic manner how effective we feel these meetings are. Are they effective or ineffective? The next index (the Task/Relationship Index) gives you the opportunity to consider one way in which meetings can be assessed. Consider either a specific meeting or a normal work meeting, and allocate a score on the scale below to each of the statements:

1	2	3	4	5
Not at all	Occasionally	A fair amount	A considerable amount	A great deal

Statements	*Score T*	*Score R*
(a) The meeting helped me understand the job we are doing more clearly.	_____	_____
(b) I learned a lot about peoples' attitudes during the meeting.		_____

Statements	Score T	Score R
(c) It was a useful meeting insofar as people got to know each other.		————
(d) It was a meeting in which I had to use my knowledge and skills.	————	
(e) People built on each other's ideas.		————
(f) Ideas were expressed freely.		————
(g) The technical content of the discussion was of a high level.	————	
(h) People kept to the point and did not waste time.	————	
(i) The decision-making process was fair.	————	
(j) Each item on the agenda received sufficient time.	————	
(k) There was a high degree of honesty and openness in the conversation.		————
(l) The acceptability of decisions was high.		————
(m) Problems were carefully diagnosed.	————	
(n) Creative solutions to problems were developed.	————	
(o) Solutions to problems were carefully assessed.	————	
(p) Differences of opinion were thoroughly discussed.		————
(q) The meeting was well organized.	————	
(r) The decision taken was of a high quality.	————	
(s) Everyone in the meeting received a fair hearing.		————
(t) The purpose of the meeting was clear.	————	
(u) Objectives were clearly established during the meeting.	————	

Statements	*Score T*	*Score R*
(v) I felt satisfied that I had an opportunity to influence the decision taken.		_____
(w) Time was used to the best advantage.	_____	
Totals	_____	_____

Scoring the Index

Meetings require two essential components to be successful. There is a need for *the task* or technical aspect, which includes the knowledge, ideas, and structural arrangements for getting work done; and *the relationship* or behavioral aspect, which includes the way people treated each other. This would involve the extent to which they helped or hindered, competed or cooperated, gave information, asked questions, and generally behaved in such a way as to work together.

The index has items on both these aspects. The Task aspect has been coded *T* and the Relationship aspect has been coded *R*. The maximum Task score was 70, and the maximum Relationship score was 50.

Use of the Task/Relationship Index

To improve managerial meetings, it is important to get feedback on key issues. This index provides a vehicle for discussing such key issues. It can be used in the following ways.

1. *Review of team meetings.* It is difficult in the day-to-day management of a team to get time to review how effective meetings are. However, if we can improve our meetings, then the time saved will more than make up for that spent in review. Sometimes such reviews can be done informally. However, where a guide is required, the *Task/Relationship Index* provides a useful basis for discussion.

It is suggested that each person be asked to nominate the top two-rated items and the lowest two-rated items and for these to be displayed. Each person is then asked to outline why he chose these items and to suggest alternative action next time where appropriate. This approach ensures that both highlights as well as weak points get aired.

The emphasis should be on improvement. Therefore it is useful to set an objective question, such as, "How can we improve our next meeting?" The information gained on the index can then be used. Those with low scores can say what they wish to have changed. Those with high scores can say what they wish to retain. In this way, a positive review can be held and ideas for improving future meetings developed.

2. *Checklist for discussion.* When managers are on a training program, it is helpful to provide a checklist against which they can discuss their own managerial meetings. This list can be used to establish a discussion about particular meetings that managers have run, with a view to developing ideas for improvement.

3. *Business exercises.* Again on training programs, managers are often asked to head a business exercise. A most valuable part of the exercise is the way the manager guides the discussion. He and the other members can learn a lot from the process. However, there needs to be an index against which people can make an assessment. Again, this index provides such a basis for discussion.

WHAT DO WE KNOW ABOUT GROUPS?

The work done by social psychologists on groups and how they work is voluminous. It is not my intention here to go through it blow by blow. However, I do think it useful to mention some of the findings which can be of interest and help managers in their day-to-day work.

Professor Norman Maier,[1] a world authority on problem solving in groups, wrote an article called "Assets and Liabilities in Group Problem Solving," in which he made the following points:

1. "The skill of the leader requires his ability to create a climate for disagreement which will permit innovation without risking hard feelings."

2. "When the discussion leader aids the consideration of several aspects of the problem-solving process and delays the solution mindedness of the group, solution quality and acceptance improve."
3. "Problem-solving activity includes searching, trying out ideas on one another, listening to understand rather than to refute, making relatively short speeches, and reacting to differences in opinion as stimulating."
4. "For a participative group to work the leader must concentrate on the group process, listen in order to understand rather than to appraise or refute, assume responsibility for accurate communication between members, be sensitive to unexpressed feelings, protect minority points of view, keep the discussion moving, and develop skills in summarizing."

These are key points, but in my experience too often ignored. Chairing a meeting is a difficult job and requires both task and relationship skills.

Maier has identified the following principles to aid creative problem solving in managerial meetings:

Principle 1: Success in problem solving requires that effort be directed toward overcoming surmountable obstacles.

Principle 2: Available facts should be used even when they are inadequate.

Principle 3: The starting point of a problem is richest in solution possibilities.

Principle 4: Problem mindedness should be increased while solution mindedness is delayed.

Principle 5: Disagreement can lead to either hard feelings or to innovation, depending on the discussion leader.

Principle 6: The idea-getting process should be separated from the idea evaluation process, because the latter inhibits the former.

Principle 7: Choice situations should be turned into problem situations.

Principle 8:   Problem situations should be turned into choice situations.

Principle 9:   Solutions suggested by the leader are improperly evaluated and tend either to be accepted or rejected.

These principles are valuable guidelines to all managers concerned to get effective decisions from groups. They are the principles which give life to Maier's simple but essential formula that:

Effective Decisions (ED) are a function (f) of the Quality (Q)
times the Acceptability (A) of the solution $ED = f(Q \times A)$

All managers have to obtain sufficient quality of information to make a good decision. However, it must be examined in terms of its acceptability to those who will implement it. Therefore, each manager in a meeting needs to consider what sort of a problem he has and what degree of acceptability is required. A simple model to picture this is shown below.

		Quality of solution required:	
		Low	*High*
Degree of acceptability required of those implementing decisions	High	Agreement needed but technical factors unimportant	Technical excellence and unanimity needed
	Low	Quick decision possible	Probable need for experts but not much discussion by others

Formulas like this are interesting but they don't solve problems. Only people meeting and agreeing to act in a particular way can do that. However, too many of our meetings are not adequately managed. The *Task/Relationship Index,* given earlier in this chapter, provides one way in which you can check your own meetings. Beyond this, consider the answers to the following questions when you next call a meeting.

What do I want the meeting to accomplish?

Are decisions going to be made?

If decisions are made, what is the method of making them?

Who should be invited?

On what basis do you *not* invite other people?

What preparation should I make and what preparation should I ask others to make for the meeting?

These are key questions to guide the pre-planning of an effective meeting. The actual meeting itself will be hard to predict. It will be like a football match, with some people attacking, others defending, and perhaps some playing for time. It is useful, however, to have a chairman or referee, however lightly he may wish to operate. At least people have a reference point in case of dispute. It is also useful to have someone who keeps the minutes, although at informal gatherings each person will probably act as his own secretary.

BEHAVIORS AT MEETINGS

It is difficult to tell what produces an effective meeting. Neil Rackham,[2] however, has spent a lot of time "counting behaviors." In particular, he observes the number of times a person "gives" information and the number of times he or she "seeks" information. Rackham has suggested that the following categories of behaviors account for what goes on beneath the words at any gathering.

Seeking behaviors
  Seeking suggestions
  Seeking clarifications

Seeking reactions
Seeking agreements/disagreements

Giving behaviors
  Telling suggestions
  Building
  Supporting
  Stating difficulty/disagreement/criticism

Now the critical behavior, according to Rackham, is the ability to build upon what others have said. Too often a statement made by one person is countered by another like, "I disagree," or "Yes, but . . . ," or "With respect . . ." A successful meeting depends upon people building on each other's information and ideas.

An example of this is when a person responds by saying, "If we take that idea you have put forward, John, and link it to the suggestion made by Ann, then we could use our new trucks to move the machinery and speed up the opening of our new office by about a month." Here the speaker seeks to build on previous contributions and link them to his own. This is an important skill. It emphasizes the positive. It is future-oriented. It looks for action which is related to other people's ideas.

However, in real life not everyone does agree with everyone else. The important thing for you as the manager is to sit back and try to see the connections. Don't jump in too early with your solution. The meeting can easily become "How can we defeat the manager's idea?" rather than "How can we get the best idea?" So your role is often better played as a catalyst, whereby you draw out other people's ideas and link them together to produce ideas everyone feels committed to make work.

Finally, if things are not going well, start asking questions rather than making statements. In this way, you will encourage people in the meeting to focus on the problems, rather than just knocking down each other's solutions. Often arguments occur because there has not been a consensus on problem definition. Spend a lot of time on that. Solutions often follow as a natural process.

THE FIVE MAIN KINDS OF MEETINGS

It is important to know what kind of meeting you are running or contributing to. Here are the main options:

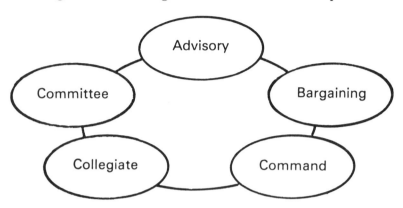

A Command Meeting

A command meeting is called by the manager to instruct or direct his subordinates to undertake a specified task or establish rules governing future behavior. The manager makes the decisions in such meetings and is accountable for the results. He decides who shall attend the meeting, what the objectives shall be, and how the work is to be achieved. The approach is therefore authoritarian, and for this form of decision making to succeed the manager needs to have the knowledge necessary to make a high-quality decision, and the knowledge that his commands will be obeyed and implemented. This approach is characteristic of military organizations and was characteristic of many business organizations in the nineteenth and early twentieth centuries. However, this type of meeting is decreasing in importance in business organizations for a number of reasons, such as the increase of professionals in organizations and the complexity of knowledge, high levels of employment, and the rise in democratic values.

An Advisory Meeting

An advisory meeting is called for the exchange of information. It is not a decision-making meeting. The information, once exchanged, is taken away by those involved and decisions on the next steps to be taken are made. An example of an advisory meeting might be a selection interview, where both parties ask for and receive information and at a subsequent date make a decision. An advisory meeting is, therefore, in essence a consultative relationship. A manager may call an advisory meeting either to inform his subordinates about ideas he has for the future or to ask their view relating to a problem. Further examples are when a manager informs his subordinates of company plans to launch new projects, to enter new markets, or to relate matters affecting them which have come up during the manager's attendance at another meeting. Again, the manager might call an advisory meeting when he requires information from subordinates or colleagues, even though they do not necessarily need to be involved in the decision made. Likewise, subordinates can also ask for an advisory meeting to gain information which will help them either to resolve problems or to make strategic decisions.

Advisory meetings, therefore, are concerned with the sharing of facts and opinions. In reality, these meetings happen all the time, mostly on an informal basis. For example, if someone says "Can you tell me . . . ?" or "What is your view on . . . ?" or "How can I get . . . ?" then it is likely that an advisory meeting has begun. At the more formal level, advisory meetings will take the form of consultative discussions or interviews.

A Collegiate Meeting

A collegiate meeting is held between people of similar status and/or professional knowledge and skill. Each person in such a meeting will have respect for the integrity of a professional opinion.

Attendance at collegiate meetings is usually based upon the fact that those present have some professional knowledge or skill to contribute to the solution of a problem and implementation of the solution. *Decisions in such meetings are usually made by consensus.* If a person disagrees at any point, it is incumbent upon him to make clear his reasons and work toward the generation of an alternative proposition that would be acceptable to all. For example, in a meeting on the construction of a bridge, there needs to be a consensus among the engineers, the accountant, and others on the basic issues. If, for example, the accountant informed the engineer that the bridge proposed was too costly in terms of the other commitments of the company, a joint reappraisal would need to be done. It would be inappropriate in such circumstances for the engineer to ignore the accountant. It would be equally inappropriate for the accountant to disregard the engineer's opinion on the necessary resources to build a safe bridge. Accountability for decisions taken lies with the collegiate body. The collegiate meeting is becoming more important as the number of professional service advisers in companies grows.

A Committee Meeting

A committee meeting is one in which representatives from various groups meet to make decisions on matters of mutual interest. Decisions in a committee are usually made by voting: those having the majority win the issue. Where there is a tie, the chairman usually decides the issue by casting his vote. The committee is the traditional democratic approach to decision making. Attendance at such meetings is usually based on one's representative role or interest in the topics being discussed. One may represent either others or oneself. Accountability for the decisions taken lies with the group, rather than any particular individual, although the danger is that only those in the majority on any given issue will give support to its implementation.

A Negotiation Meeting

A negotiation meeting has similarities to a committee meeting, but decisions are made more on a quid pro quo basis, rather than voting. Each side will have different objectives but mutual interests arising from interdependence. Each side seeks to achieve the best terms, and decisions are made in relation to supply and demand factors. Decisions in such meetings are joint, and both sides are expected to support the implementation of the decision, if only to fulfill their own interests.

The above description of meetings together with the approaches to problem solving are extended further in my previous book.[3]

SUMMARY

This chapter has provided an index to measure the effectiveness of work meetings. In addition, some important research findings have been reviewed. These together with the description of the meetings mentioned above provide guidelines on how we can think about meetings in a positive way. However, meetings are essentially about people. Bringing people together inevitably means a contrast, if not a conflict, of views. The skill of managing the resolution of different opinions and obtaining commitment to effective action is the main asset of a good manager. The ideas here provide guidelines. The rest is part of the action, and this will test your practical skills as well as your theory. By reviewing the action with those involved you can seek ways of improving the effectiveness of your meeting.

In my role as the chairman of meetings, my strengths are:

_____

_____

_____

_____

To improve my performance as the leader of meetings I should:

_____

_____

_____

_____

To improve the work of our meetings my group should:

_____

_____

_____

"Visual aids are vital to effective problem solving"
In your meetings as a manager, what preparations do you make for enabling ideas and contributions to be made visible and managed against a time schedule? Below are some obvious examples against which you can check your own meetings and add on others which could help the process of debate.

Overhead projector _____

Flip charts _____

Marker pens _____

Reports _____

Financial statements _____

Table layout—square, circular,
   diagonal, rectangular _____

A clock _____

Written agenda _____

Minutes _____

Models and diagrams _____

"Ideas get lost unless they are written down"

NOTES

1. Maier, N.F.R., "Assets and Liabilities in Group Problem Solving," *Psychological Review,* Vol. 74, No. 4, 1967.
   —*Problem-Solving Discussions and Conferences* (New York: McGraw-Hill, 1963).
2. Rackham, N., and Morgan, T., *Behaviour Analysis in Training* (London: McGraw-Hill, 1976).
3. Margerison, C., *Managerial Problem Solving* (New York: McGraw-Hill, 1976).

CHAPTER 7

Are you an entrepreneur?

WE WANT MEN IN THIS COMPANY WITH INITIATIVE, CREATIVITY, INDEPENDENCE, ENTREPRENEURSHIP, A WILL TO GET AHEAD AND ABOVE ALL, YOU MUST BE A SELF-STARTER.

YES, THAT'S ME. I'LL TAKE THE JOB.

THEN SHUT UP, SIT STILL, AND LISTEN CAREFULLY TO WHAT I WANT YOU TO DO.

WHO MAKES IT?

WE HAVE ALL HEARD STORIES of how individuals made fortunes. Were they lucky or did they have a special ability? The rags-to-riches road usually involves both. However, most of those people who succeed say they made their own luck.

"Entrepreneur" has become a term to describe those who succeed in developing new business opportunities. It is a wide term covering street vendors, asset strippers,* property developers, wheeler-dealers, financial wizards, enterprising executives, and well-established directors of businesses.

Typically, our culture is somewhat ambivalent about entrepreneurs. On the one hand, we like them because they introduce glamour, excitement, and new vistas of opportunity. However, we also consider such people to be potential sharks, in for the quick rip-off, and exploiting others and the environment to their own advantage.

Nevertheless, our society needs people with enterprise if we are to improve the quality and quantity of our life. It is here that the real dilemma about entrepreneurs occurs. Ideally, we would like our entrepreneurs to be socially responsible and do things for the public good as well as for personal gain.

In this section we shall, therefore, look at entrepreneurs and what is meant by entrepreneurial activity. Before you assess your own entrepreneurial ability, consider the following list of people. How would you rate them

As entrepreneurs?

As socially responsible?

As to your willingness to work with them?

Please give a score from the following scale:

*"Asset strippers" are people who take over companies not for investment purposes but to extract anything of value from the companies.

86

1	2	3	4	5
Very low	Low	Medium	High	Very high

Entre-preneurs	Organization	Entre-preneurial score	Social re-sponsibility score	Willingness to work for score
William Hesketh Lever	Unilever			
Edwin H. Land	Polaroid			
Thomas Watson	International Business Machines			
Bernard Cornfeld	Investors Overseas Service			
Freddie Laker	Laker Airlines			
Henry Ford I	Ford Motor Company			

Clearly, from your answers, you have views about entrepreneurs and the way they operate. It is also clear that it is difficult to say all entrepreneurs are the same. However, research shows that there are certain factors that tend to be associated with entrepreneurial behavior.

The remainder of this chapter gives you the opportunity to assess your own inclination and entrepreneurial activity. Following this, there is a brief review of some of the research findings and their implications. The *Self-Assessment Index* is based upon issues that have been identified from studies of a large number of entrepreneurs. Clearly, not all entrepreneurs can be defined in a similar way. The material presented here represents, therefore, some behaviors and characteristics that have been found to recur a number of times in the lives of many entrepreneurs.

THE ENTREPRENEUR'S SELF-ASSESSMENT INDEX

This index gives you an opportunity to assess yourself on a number of criteria related to entrepreneurship. It is not a test. The items referred to in the index have been drawn from research studies. Most of them are highly related to characteristics of entrepreneurs. Other of the points in the index indicate the relationships with people exhibited by those who have shown entrepreneurial ability. An explanation of the index and your total entrepreneurial score will be given at the end.

For the time being, please go through the items mentioned and allocate a score on the scale as shown below:

1	2	3	4	5
Very low	Low	Medium	High	Very high

Please circle the number which is most appropriate to your own situation for each item. At the end, you can then draw a line through these points to get an overall profile. In addition, you will have the opportunity to add the scores up and measure your self-assessed entrepreneurial approach.

SECTION 1—How Others See Me

Please circle the appropriate score

I am a person whom others find . . . .

(a) difficult to organize.	1	2	3	4	5
(b) a powerful influence.	1	2	3	4	5
(c) a person of doubtful conscience.	1	2	3	4	5
(d) more anxious than average.	1	2	3	4	5
(e) keen always to explore new ideas.	1	2	3	4	5
(f) difficult to understand.	1	2	3	4	5
(g) different or even "way out."	1	2	3	4	5
(h) somewhat impulsive.	1	2	3	4	5
(i) somewhat unstable.	1	2	3	4	5

Section 1 total _____

SECTION 2—Personal Perspective

I feel that I am inclined . . . .

(a) to panic a bit when I have too
much success.   1   2   3   4   5

(b) to prefer a benevolent-dictator
style of managing.   1   2   3   4   5

(c) to be uncomfortable when working for someone else.   1   2   3   4   5

(d) to be anxious about making
things happen.   1   2   3   4   5

(e) to feel somewhat destructive at
times.   1   2   3   4   5

(f) to value achievement more than
power.   1   2   3   4   5

(g) to act on my intuition and feel of
the situations rather than plan
carefully.   1   2   3   4   5

Section 2 total _____

SECTION 3—Beliefs

I believe that . . . .

(a) I can materially influence the
direction of a business.   1   2   3   4   5

(b) I am lucky.   1   2   3   4   5

(c) I can cope well with unforeseen
troubles when they occur.   1   2   3   4   5

(d) I am an optimist.   1   2   3   4   5

(e) I am self-reliant.   1   2   3   4   5

(f) I like dealing with ambiguous work
problems.   1   2   3   4   5

(g) I reject the conventional way of
doing things.   1   2   3   4   5

Section 3 total _____

SECTION 4—Preferences

I prefer to work in such a way that . . . .

(a) it enables me to take a commercial risk where I can make or lose money.	1	2	3	4	5
(b) the risks go just beyond my personal experience.	1	2	3	4	5
(c) I know quickly whether the risks have paid off.	1	2	3	4	5
(d) I am in touch with market opportunities.	1	2	3	4	5
(e) it achieves results at a profit.	1	2	3	4	5
(f) I am in control of the business.	1	2	3	4	5

Section 4 total _____

SECTION 5—Characteristics

I am the sort of person who . . . .

(a) rarely plans ahead in a logical way.	1	2	3	4	5
(b) is not too worried about getting colleagues and subordinates to agree with me before I act.	1	2	3	4	5
(c) doesn't like to write things down too much.	1	2	3	4	5
(d) is unlikely to conform with other people's views very much on what should be done.	1	2	3	4	5
(e) usually dislikes dealing with details of a technical nature in business matters.	1	2	3	4	5
(f) tends to neglect interpersonal relationships at work and offend people from time to time.	1	2	3	4	5
(g) finds it difficult to be orderly, neat, and tidy at work.	1	2	3	4	5

(h) expects business ventures to fail
from time to time, but will have
another go.   1   2   3   4   5

(i) enjoys the excitement, adventure,
and danger of failure in
taking business risks.   1   2   3   4   5

Section 5 total _____

SECTION 6—Relationships

I consider that . . . .

(a) I have more respect for my
mother than for my father.   1   2   3   4   5

(b) my mother was a strong influence
on my approach to business.   1   2   3   4   5

(c) I am self-willed.   1   2   3   4   5

(d) I have few strong personal
loyalties.   1   2   3   4   5

(e) other people are too security-
conscious.   1   2   3   4   5

(f) I can succeed in business where
others fail.   1   2   3   4   5

(g) I don't trust people too much.   1   2   3   4   5

(h) I know how to influence people
in business.   1   2   3   4   5

Section 6 total _____

Overall Score

Section 1	
Section 2	
Section 3	
Section 4	
Section 5	
Section 6	
Total	

HOW DID YOU SCORE?

The *Entrepreneurial Self-Assessment Index* gives you a guide based upon the available evidence as to the characteristics associated with a number of entrepreneurs. Clearly, this doesn't describe every entrepreneur. However, it does represent a good cross section of people who have succeeded or failed as entrepreneurs.

A high score on each of the items would be associated with the characteristics expected of many entrepreneurs. Therefore, if you got a score of 150 or more overall, then it is highly likely that you will have an inclination toward entrepreneurial activity. Those who scored between 120 and 150 will indeed be enterprising, but not necessarily as dedicated and committed to outright entrepreneurship as others. Those scoring between 80 and 120 will have some innovative and enterprising characteristics but are unlikely to have the outright determination to succeed as entrepreneurs. Those scoring below 80 will prefer a much more secure type of job and wish to exercise influence in a different way.

It is interesting today that we are seeing perhaps a different kind of entrepreneur develop. This sort of person is more a careerist. We give the name "manager" or "executive" to many people who exercise a high degree of business acumen but within an organization which they themselves did not found. These managerial entrepreneurs, however, do exercise a high degree of initiative and enterprise in pushing their organizations to very great heights.

Not all entrepreneurs are buccaneers. A number of them have very strong consciences and seek to use their enterprises for improving the lot of others. A notable example of this was W.H. Lever. Besides founding the organization which gave rise to Unilever, he was in fact a major philanthropist. Wherever he went, he designed communities where his workers could live in good conditions. In addition, he emphasized the importance of providing good working conditions so that people had dignity and respect. This approach was characteristic also of other enlightened entrepreneurs such as Cadbury's in Britain.

In contrast, a number of entrepreneurs have been self-centered and have exploited other people for their own advantage. It has been said that many of the founders of the Industrial Revolution in Britain had this approach, and many of the fortunes that were gained in the textile and iron industries were based upon master/servant relationships, which had employees, including young children, working for long hours in appalling conditions. The history of Britain, among other countries, is littered with terrible examples of people working in subhuman conditions in mines and factories, under the entrepreneurial management of people whose only interest was in their own gain.

In an interesting 1977 article, Kets de Vries[1] says that entrepreneurs have a high need for achievement and, in particular, "need for autonomy, independence, and moderate risk taking." He goes on to suggest, "The entrepreneur also emerges as an anxious individual, a nonconformist, poorly organized and not a stranger to self-destructive behavior." They seem to be "inner directed" and, moreover, "to present themselves as self-reliant and tend to de-emphasize or neglect interpersonal relations."

It would appear that entrepreneurs like their own way, often even if it means on a road to failure. It is clear that they are not necessarily likable people. They are often short on patience and understanding and indeed sometimes on charity. An entrepreneur is indeed persistent and can be a hard person to deal with in that he wishes to have his own way. He will often push past or trample over people to get what he wants, perhaps apologizing after he has succeeded. Indeed, many entrepreneurs in their latter years become somewhat benevolent and give back much of their wealth to good causes. However, they would go along in most cases with the expression "Nice guys finish last," and justify their actions in terms of success.

SO ARE YOU REALLY AN ENTREPRENEUR?

In most of us, there is the desire to run our own show. However, equally we recognize the difficulty of doing so. To become an entrepreneur involves a high degree of risk taking and determination to succeed. You may, therefore, consider to what extent you really do wish to be an entrepreneur.

1. If I became an entrepreneur what sort of business would I set up?

_____

_____

_____

_____

2. What do I feel are the personal characteristics in me that would enable me to make a success as an entrepreneur?

_____

_____

_____

_____

3. What are the personal characteristics I have that are likely to make it difficult for me to be an entrepreneur?

_____

_____

_____

_____

4. If I wish to start as an entrepreneur, what must I do in the next twelve months?

_____

_____

_____

_____

These are some of the questions which you should ask yourself if you are seriously considering setting up your own business. However, beyond this it is possible, as we have indicated, to be a managerial entrepreneur. This is a route which many people are taking. Having identified your situation, you may feel that being a managerial entrepreneur would be more appropriate. If so, consider the following questions.

1. What position in an organization do I need to obtain to be a managerial entrepreneur?

_____

_____

_____

_____

2. What are the advantages of being a managerial entrepreneur in a large organization?

_____

_____

_____

_____

3. What are the disadvantages of being a managerial entrepreneur in a large organization?

_____

_____

_____

_____

4. What steps should I take to further my chances of becoming a managerial entrepreneur?

_____

_____

_____

_____

When all is said and done, entrepreneurship demands a high degree of intuitive understanding of business. It is not something which people can systemically work out. You either feel the need to express your abilities in an entrepreneurial way, or you opt for a more stable approach to earning a living. Where do you stand? What do you intend to do? There are still many opportunities for entrepreneurs both in large organizations and in running your own business. It's up to you what is the best course of action.

NOTE

1. Kets de Vries, M.F.R., "The Entrepreneurial Personality: A Person at the Crossroads," *Journal of Management Studies,* Vol. 14, No. 1, 1977.

REFERENCES

Bruce, R. *The Entrepreneurs.* London: Libertarian Books, 1976.

Collins, O., et al. *The Organisation Makers.* London: Appleton-Century-Crofts, 1970.

Lynn, R. *The Entrepreneur.* New York: Beekman, 1974.

CHAPTER 8

Do you work under pressure?

HOW IS PRESSURE CREATED?

"IN THIS JOB you've got to run fast just to keep up with yourself." It's a point of view that is increasingly heard these days. Given that we have so many labor-saving devices such as cars, telephones, washing machines, electric mowers, and escalators, we still seem to be under pressure.

Is it we, the job, or other people who create the pressure? Maybe it's a mixture of all three. If you feel under pressure, then this section is of particular importance to you.

Pressure has been accused of contributing to heart attacks. The dreaded coronary disease is well on the way to claiming more than a million American victims a year. Now they are not necessarily all victims of pressure and stress, but there is increasing concern that many such deaths are dramatically affected by this factor, particularly if one is not fit and tends to overeat.

To what extent do you feel under pressure at work and in life generally? Pressure is a difficult thing to measure in any precise form. We all know when we are under heavy pressure, for we begin to feel physically as well as mentally tired. However, it is often hard to pinpoint the exact cause.

Dr. Malcolm Carruthers[1] has suggested that it is the emotional stresses of modern life that really create the key source of coronary illness. Often, it is the stress engendered by the job which is the important factor, as with bus drivers and airline pilots. However, we also need to look at the type of person we are and ask, "Am I easily upset and subject to stress?"

LIFE AND WORK INDEX

To start with, therefore, let us assess the situation as you see it. The following index asks a number of questions about you and your job. Give an honest-to-goodness answer, even if you know it will register high or low on the index counter. You can mislead the questionnaire, but you can't mislead yourself.

Read the statements, then score yourself using a scale of 1 to 10, with 1 = never and 10 = always. The maximum possible total score is 100.

	My score
1. I like to crowd lots of activities into each day.	_____
2. If I make an error or mistake in my job, the consequences are likely to be very serious, particularly in terms of people's safety.	_____
3. My life is a continual fight to meet deadlines and targets within a limited time.	_____
4. I recognize that I can be quick-tempered.	_____
5. I feel uneasy if I am just relaxing and doing nothing in particular.	_____
6. My job demands a hostile, aggressive style and approach	_____
7. I feel tense at work quite a lot.	_____
8. Generally, I am more concerned with planning and preparing for the future than with taking time out to relax.	_____
9. One of my major concerns is how I can move faster so that I can do more things in less time.	_____
10. I make sure on most occasions that things are done my way.	_____
	Total _____

This measure is based upon factors which Drs. Friedman and Rosenman[2] outlined in their research. They concluded that there are two major types of people. These they referred to as Type A and Type B people.

Type A people were defined as being most competitive, always seeking new targets, desiring action, working to meet deadlines, often aggressive and bad-tempered, concerned with planning ahead, and generally crowding lots of activities into a busy schedule. In short, they were people who had a sense of urgency.

Type B people were defined as more easygoing, taking difficulties in their stride without getting unduly flustered or upset, working steadily, and generally taking their time and maintaining a balanced schedule of events for the space available.

Now if you got a high score on the Life and Work Index, you are clearly more of a Type A person than a Type B. The implications can be important. For example, two groups living in the same community, eating similar food, and smoking at about the same levels were compared. It was found that Type A people had about six times as many heart attacks as Type B people. So where do you stand?

My own studies show the following self-rated scores for 126 managers from many jobs, including chemical engineers, bankers, salesmen, and production people. The words in the left-hand column reflect the key word for each of the questions numbered as before, respectively 1 to 10.

	Mean score
1. Activities	6.24
2. Mistakes	5.66
3. Deadlines	5.87
4. Quick temper	4.70
5. Relaxation	6.06
6. Aggression	3.33
7. Tenseness	4.30
8. Work orientation	6.63
9. Speed	5.64
10. Job control	6.07

In addition, there are the range scores. Here 91 individual totals were compared to see what the lowest third, the middle third, and the top third looked like. Here are the scores:

Top third	60.5 –73.75
Middle third	51.0 –57.75
Bottom third	34.75–46.25

This should give you an indication of how much pressure you feel under, compared to other people in managerial positions. However, comparison will not in itself decide whether you are under pressure or not. Only you will know this. What is too much pressure for one person is not enough for another, and vice versa.

So pressure can be dangerous. But it needs to be seen in its work and life context. An excellent summary of the research on this has been given by French and Caplan.[3] They show that there are a variety of stresses leading to coronary heart disease. These appear on the following pages. The authors summarize their findings by saying, "It is the responsibility which organizational members have for other organizational members, rather than the responsibility for impersonal aspects of the organization, which constitutes the more significant organizational stress."

Is this true in your job? What has caused you stress during the last six months?

_____

_____

_____

_____

_____

What did you do to resolve the matter?

_____

_____

_____

_____

_____

> **What Sort of Person You Are**
> Abilities vs. Needs
> Introverted vs. Extroverted
> Flexible vs. Rigid

> **Do You Fit Your Job?**
> Degree of role clarity required and provided
> Degree of role conflict required and provided
> Degree of workload required and provided
> Extent to which your crossing organizational boundaries creates stress
> Extent to which your responsibility for people creates stress
> Extent to which your need to relate to others creates stress
> Extent to which your need to participate creates stress

> **Signs of Stress**
> Job dissatisfaction
> Job tensions
> Low self-actualization
> High smoking
> High blood pressure
> High cholesterol
> High heart rate
> Low self-esteem

Now let us look at the wider aspect of prevention and reduction of stress at work and in life.

SO WHAT CAN YOU DO?

We all have pressure upon us. Indeed, without it I expect little would get done. Moderate pressure is energizing and encourages people to perform at their best. Clearly, pressure of the appropriate amount at the appropriate time is a good thing.

But if the pressure is getting to be too much, then action is necessary to remedy the situation. Well, here is where you can think it through. Below is a wheel of opportunity. All you have to do is examine the options open to you to reduce, eliminate, or divert the unwanted pressure you are under. I have filled in some fairly obvious possibilities and I leave you to consider what others are possible for you.

ARE YOU FIT TO MANAGE?

No doubt you have mentioned physical exercise and fitness in your list. Here are some typical comments made by managers when I asked them how they keep physically fit. How far do similar comments apply to you?

"I play golf once a week, except, of course, when the weather is bad."

"I have deliberately not bought a power mower. I feel that pushing the old hand mower is important, as it keeps me in condition."

"Yes, I keep fit for work by running up the steps to my office three or four times a day. It used to take my breath away, but I can do it now without too much effort."

"Exercise is a good idea, provided you don't overdo it. I do a bit of arm stretching and a few pushups every week. I think that is enough, don't you?"

Well, is it enough? Maybe you can add the fact that you walk a quarter of a mile to the train each day, or maybe you go for a walk on the weekend and possibly even play tennis or badminton once a week.

If you do, then you are an honest tryer. But honestly trying without a plan is not sufficient. You are shooting in the dark. You hope you are doing enough to stay fit, but in honesty you cannot be sure you have done enough.

Our research into managerial fitness covers three major aspects, of which physical fitness is only one part. We feel that a manager, like any other worker, must develop and maintain his fitness on three levels.

Physical fitness means the manager's ability to maintain his body in a condition that will enable him to do his job without disability arising from physical ill health.

Mental fitness refers to the knowledge that a manager requires to do his job, plus the frame of mind that enables him to cope with stress.

Task fitness refers to the skills a manager requires, both at the technical and interpersonal levels, to deal with his job.

Now it is a point of some significance that while managers spend countless hours evaluating and measuring the condition of the business, they spend relatively little time measuring and evaluating their own managerial fitness. To measure costs, count revenue, draft budgets, use techniques to assess cash flow, work out depreciation, calculate investment, and eventually count profit are all part of managerial work. When the figures are not known or are out of line with budgets there is a hue and cry.

THE INDIVIDUAL BALANCE SHEET

But what about you? Do you know how to measure yourself? What does your individual balance sheet look like? Our evidence suggests that hardly any managers do conduct other than cursory measures. Most are based more on feelings than facts. Few know how to conduct measures of their fitness.

So the standards we apply to our business assessments we do not seem to apply to ourselves. I believe it is vitally important that managers have measures and standards which they can use to assess their managerial fitness. Moreover, these measures should give early warning for action. Just as a company wants to know when it is running out of cash, so a manager should know when he is in need of preventive or remedial help.

The chart below is a quick guide. Find out where you fall by marking a point on each axis and plotting a square.

If you find yourself in Section A, then watch out. This

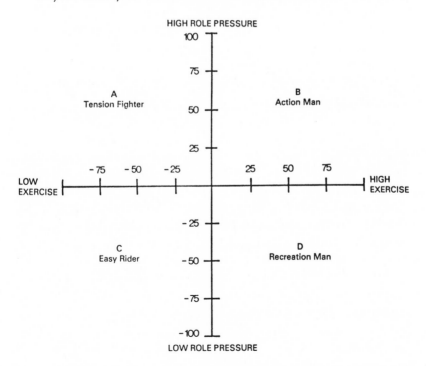

could be a dangerous situation. Low exercise and high job pressure produce a potentially lethal condition.

Section B means that you at least are taking some positive steps, but are they enough? The next part of this chapter will give you some guidelines on what level of exercise is appropriate.

Section C sounds like an easy life. Perhaps it's too easy. Certainly, to increase the exercise level is usually beneficial, provided you do it gradually. I'll leave it to you to judge if the job needs changing.

Section D seems a good position for reducing the risk. High exercise and low job pressure seem a sensible combination. Few people these days, however, have such a position.

HOW IMPORTANT IS EXERCISE?

There have been a number of important studies to see if physical exercise has an effect on people having heart attacks. It would seem clear that physical exercise has a beneficial effect. All the studies show that people who have jobs where they are engaged in physical work, or who take deliberate steps to engage in physical exercises, are less likely to have heart attacks.

Here is a quick review of some of the most famous studies.

London Transport

A study of 31,000 people aged between 35 and 64 was undertaken, comparing bus drivers and bus conductors. During the course of one year, 2.7 per 1,000 of the drivers, as compared to 1.9 per 1,000 of the conductors, had heart attacks. Indeed, the drivers had over twice as many "rapidly fatal" attacks as did the conductors.

The Post Office and Civil Service

This study was done on men between the ages of 35 and 59, comparing postmen with telephonists and clerks. Again, the postmen do a more physically active job than the clerks, and the results are similar to the drivers and conductors study. The clerks had 2.4 heart attacks per 1,000 people, and the postmen 1.8 per 1,000. Again, the "rapidly fatal" figures were twice as high for the sedentary workers.

Dock Workers

A long-term study has shown that dock workers engaged in high physical activity have a far lower coronary heart disease rate than those in less demanding jobs. This study, done in San Francisco between 1951 and 1972, studied 6,000 dock workers. The heavy physical work group had 26.9 heart attacks per 10,000 workyears, compared to 49.0 for workers with low physical activity.

Framingham

This well-known study took place in a town in Massachusetts. Over a period of ten years, 207 of the 5,000 people experienced some kind of heart attack. It was clear that those in the most sedentary jobs had coronary incidence almost twice that of those who were "moderately active."

WHAT CAN BE DONE?

Recently, there have been a considerable number of publications outlining practical approaches to finess. One of the best was printed in the *Sunday Times* (London) on November 21, 1976. This has subsequently been issued as a book. The ideas put forward give a wide indication of how to test yourself and take physical exercise to maintain fitness.

Another interesting study has been made by Blythe and published in the *New Scientist,* May 6, 1976, dealing with our eating habits, and identifying foods which are associated with heart disease.

A number of books are useful as guidelines, and I have listed some of the more important ones at chapter's end.

ACTION PLAN

Now that you have identified areas for action, you need a plan of campaign. Good intentions by themselves are not sufficient. To be effective, set yourself targets.

For example, if you decide to start jogging, then have a program of activity. Don't try to run two or three miles at your first attempt. Indeed, it is likely to be more sensible to start by trying a brisk half-mile walk, then gradually build it up until you can run a mile or more.

The same is likely to be useful for things you wish to stop doing. For example, if you now smoke 40 cigarettes a day it will probably be difficult to stop immediately. If so, then set yourself a series of targets—say, 30 this week, 25 next, 15 the week after, and so on. Should you be able to give up the smoking habit quicker, then all the better.

Gradual steady progress is the secret in most things. The same is true in improving your own fitness. It is now accepted that we all have to be responsible for our own health. A number of books and articles are available to give guidance. I have been particularly influenced by several books by Cooper.[4] These are both well written and specifically informative on the exercises that are useful for improving fitness. The books give guidance to people of different ages on the appropriate amount of exercise, rather than general exhortation. Besides these books, there are other useful guides and I have listed a few below.

The important thing is to be persistent. People often given up something for a week or so, or go on a few jogs. The key to success is regularity. But above all, start gradually. After that, as Cooper and others have pointed out, it is possible to keep fit by physical exercise that takes up only forty to sixty minutes a week. However, this exercise is not all taken at once, and it has to be done in a planned and careful manner. So why not read and run on by having a look at the following books.

NOTES

1. Carruthers, M., *The Western Way of Death* (New York: Pantheon, 1974).
2. Friedman, M., and Rosenman, R., *Type A Behavior and Your Heart* (New York: Alfred A. Knopf, 1974).

3. French, J.P.R., and Caplan, R.D., "Organizational Stress and Individual Strain," in *The Failure of Success*, edited by A.J. Marrow (New York: AMACOM, 1967).
4. Cooper, K., *Aerobics* (New York: Bantam, 1968).
   —*The New Aerobics* (New York: Bantam, 1970).
   —*The Aerobics Way* (New York: Bantam, 1977).

REFERENCES

Bell, E. *Live Longer, Live Better*. London: Gollancz, 1975.

Buck, V. *Working Under Pressure*. London: MCB Publications, 1975.

Durrant, M. *Eat Well and Keep Healthy*. London: Macdonald Educational, 1977.

Gowler, D., and Legge, K. *Managerial Stress*. Epping, Essex: Gower Press, 1975.

CHAPTER 9

What sort of organization do you work in?

ORGANIZATIONAL IMAGES

ORGANIZATIONS, LIKE PEOPLE, have characteristics. The organizations we work in develop an overall image. People will attribute to the organization certain strengths and weaknesses. For example, you will hear people say, "That's a good organization to work for." Alternatively, you may hear people say, "I wouldn't work there the way they treat people."

Such comments are based upon an individual's perception of the organization. This is built up from a series of incidents. These may involve personal experience, hearsay, press reports, and television or other media.

Here we are concerned with how we see our present organization. We can, therefore, rely upon our experience. However, that in itself is limiting. We only see part of the organization at particular points in time. Nevertheless, it is interesting to note the degree to which people in organizations broadly agree or disagree on how they see the organization.

ASPECTS OF ORGANIZATION

Our task here is to provide a description of key aspects of the organization. This will provide the basis for discussing the culture of the organization. Just as the culture of America is different from that of India, so organizations differ. What culture exists in your organization? Is it appropriate? Does it suit your personal preference?

Again, we shall use a self-completion index. This will outline some major concepts pertaining to organizational life. Look at your own organization as you know it. Do the concepts apply? When making your judgments, keep in mind the part of the organization to which you belong. By this, I mean choose the organization (or part of it) that you feel is important. The only proviso is that you also look beyond your own immediate group, if there is considerable influence being exerted from outside. So when making a decision do not just confine it to your own team. Make an overall assessment.

For each item on this Organizational Style Index, please circle a score from the scale below which most closely corresponds with how you see your organization.

0	1	2	3
Does not describe my organization	Describes my organization a little	Describes my organization a fair amount	Describes my organization most of the time

(a) Controlling	0	1	2	3
(b) Thrusting	0	1	2	3
(c) Helpful	0	1 ·	2	3
(d) Careful	0	1	2	3
(e) Stable	0	1	2	3
(f) Entrepreneurial	0	1	2	3
(g) Exciting	0	1	2	3
(h) Secure	0	1	2	3
(i) Fair	0	1	2	3
(j) Opportunities	0	1	2	3
(k) Lots of rules	0	1	2	3
(l) Dynamic	0	1	2	3
(m) Systematic	0	1	2	3
(n) Forward-looking	0	1	2	3
(o) Organized	0	1	2	3
(p) Friendly	0	1	2	3
(q) Open	0	1	2	3
(r) Creative	0	1	2	3
(s) Ambitious	0	1	2	3
(t) Harmonious	0	1	2	3
(u) Compartmentalized	0	1	2	3
(v) Hierarchical	0	1	2	3
(w) Warm	0	1	2	3
(x) Risk taking	0	1	2	3

By drawing a line between the scores vertically, an overall profile can be gained. This can provide a basis for easy comparison between different organizations.

What the Index Assesses

The items in this index examine the extent to which you see your organization as *bureaucratic, innovative,* and *supportive.*

For the purpose of analysis you can chart your own organization on the bureaucratic, innovative, and supportive dimensions below.

Bureaucratic Profile		Innovative Profile		Supportiveness Profile	
Items	Score	Items	Score	Items	Score
a		b		c	
d		f		h	
e		g		i	
k		l		j	
m		n		p	
o		r		q	
v		s		t	
u		x		w	
Total		Total		Total	

HOW BUREAUCRATIC IS YOUR ORGANIZATION?

If you have given your organization a high score for stable, lots of rules, controlling, and organized, then it is likely you work in a bureaucratic organization. This may be a good or bad situation depending on what you want and what is appropriate to the situation. For example, if the market for your products is stable and you have a large market share, well-trained staff, and a sound structure, then a bureaucratic organization may be appropriate. However, it is unlikely to attract creative, innovative, and ambitious people to work in it.

Some departments within a large organization which itself is growing can nevertheless have a bureaucratic profile. Their job is to maintain and develop order in what can be a rapidly changing situation. Such departments find themselves under tremendous stress during such times. They try to set up systems to cope with salespeople who are introducing new orders, and research and development people introducing new ideas. It is in such situations that tension and conflict develop.

Therefore, consider what your situation is. Is the organization mainly controlled by the bureaucratic approach? Am I personally suited to a bureaucratic approach?

HOW INNOVATIVE IS YOUR ORGANIZATION?

If you have described your organization as high on creativity, thrusting, dynamic, and innovative, then the answer is clear. Such organizations are often exciting places to work in. There is also usually a high degree of optimism. Generally, people are motivated to a meaningful goal.

However, such organizations are not easy to live in. The pressure can be intense. People working in advertising agencies, for example, find them very innovative but stressful. Therefore, you need to have the personality that can cope with such a rich environment. Many people leave such organizations because they find their own personal life style doesn't fit the demands of the organization.

In theory, the bureaucratic and innovative organizations are poles apart. In reality, this is not always so. The research and development laboratory of organizations can exhibit high innovation but be subject to systematic, rational procedures and proceed optimistically but with caution.

HOW SUPPORTIVE IS YOUR ORGANIZATION?

The third major characteristic in this assessment is the extent to which you feel your organization is a reasonable place to work in. A key factor in most research is the extent to which the employee sees the organization as a supportive place. Clearly, this means in a physical sense that it provides a secure job, but the concept is deeper than this.

If you have described your organization as fair, friendly, helpful, open, warm, and harmonious, then the culture is defined as supportive. In this sense, the organization is seen as a psychologically beneficial place in which to work. It has been found that productivity at work is influenced considerably by the extent to which people feel the environment is supportive of their effort. It is obviously easier to work in such an atmosphere. However, there is little evidence to suggest that satisfaction with one's work situation in itself produces high productivity. There need to be other factors present, as indicated in Chapter 5, "What Motivates You and Others?"

Now both bureaucratic and innovative organization cultures can be supportive or alternatively lacking in support. The degree of supportiveness is largely a result of managerial practices. The manager, through his personal relations, can do a lot to foster a supportive attitude. It is not always possible for managers to influence the conditions producing the need for bureaucracy or innovation, but they can influence the degree of supportiveness.

This diagram enables you to chart the profile of your organization. To do this, take the scores from the three Profile boxes shown earlier and plot your overall organizational profile.

Bureaucratic Score	Innovative Score	Supportive Score
24– maximum	24– maximum	24– maximum
18–	18–	18–
12–	12–	12–
6–	6–	6–
0–	0–	0–

As you see, the diagram provides an opportunity to chart your organization's scores on innovation and bureaucracy against supportiveness. To do this, draw a line from the innovative score so that it meets the line coming up from the supportive and bureaucratic scores. The area covered will show the relationship between innovation and perceived supportiveness and bureaucracy.

FUTURE STEPS

The charting of organizational culture will become more important. These indexes are but simple steps on a complex road. The world of tomorrow, I believe, will require organizations to look much more closely at their culture. The recent legislation and reports on employee participation have pointed the way. All organizations will be required to give employees far more information than previously.

This information will go beyond the financial facts and figures. Employees will, I am sure, ask for assessments of what people *feel* about the organization. What is it like as a place to work in? What changes in work conditions should be made? How do departments compare on their communication practices?

Some companies already take these and similar issues very seriously. For example, IBM and Texas Instruments conduct annual surveys on attitudes within the firm and publish the results for all the staff. Many more organizations commission attitude surveys to discover what outside people think of them and their products.

There is a major development occurring in organizations on factors like participation and involvement, and this demands greater understanding of how people see their culture. The following index indicates in more depth one simple way in which we can begin to discuss such issues. It is the discussion rather than the index that is important. The index only serves to highlight some important areas. So while assessment is important, discussion is vital. However, at the end of the day action must follow to improve areas that require it. In this way, we can further the development of the organizations in which we spend so much of our lives.

RESEARCH ON ORGANIZATIONAL SURVEYS

The most well-known research is based on the sort of approach made by Rensis Likert[1] and his colleagues at the Institute for Social Research at Michigan. He chose the following factors as the basis for surveying people's opinions.

Leadership	Communication	Goals
Motivation	Decisions	Control

These factors formed the basis of a questionnaire, which was constructed on the simple scale shown here. Taking communication as an example:

	System 1:	System 2:	System 3:	System 4:
How well do superiors know the problems faced by subordinates?	Not very well	Rather well	Quite well	Very well

For simplicity Likert refers to Systems 1, 2, 3, and 4, with the latter being the ideal for which to aim. His studies show that the closer people rate their organization to System 4, the more effective it is on business and personnel criteria. Moreover, Likert argues that it is the task of managers to set the climate within which people work. Therefore, gathering such information and taking action where low scores exist is a way toward organizational improvement.

The overall measure, while being simple, is only a guide to indicate where more effort is required. It is a diagnostic tool. The data will not tell you what to do or when to do it. In this sense, the survey instrument is just like any other management information tool. However, this particular instrument is not really like other management techniques. The survey requires widespread cooperation and agreement of the staff who will provide the information. This information is their subjective impressions of how they feel about their bosses, the job, the way decisions are taken, and so forth.

Therefore, to embark on such a survey approach invariably means moving to a participative, consultative style of managing. It is little use asking people's opinions if you then ignore them. People like to get feedback. Moreover, they will expect to be consulted. So a survey cannot be seen just as another managerial tool. It is part of a managerial process.

Finally, consider the organization you work in. Is it compatible with your own needs for power, sociability, and achievement? In 1968, George Litwin and Robert Stringer[2] did some innovative work, which indicated that leadership style has a major bearing upon the overall climate and approach to work of an organization. Below are some of the key ideas that emerged. In concluding this chapter, tick off how many of these issues apply to your organization and see how compatible it is with your own preference.

Sociable Climate	Power Climate	Achievement Climate
Warm and friendly relationships	Considerable structure in jobs	Personal accountability emphasized
Support and encouragement for individuals	Lots of rules and regulations	Calculated risk and innovation encouraged
Lots of freedom for individuals	Conflict resolved by formal authority	High performance recognized
Individuals accepted into "family groups"	Systems and procedures	Little constraint on action
Personal contact important	Control and inspection important	Targets and results important

Here we have a quick check on our original scale. The Sociable Climate reflects the supportive organization. The Power Climate is clearly a reflection of the bureaucratic organization. Finally, the Achievement Climate describes major aspects of the innovative organization. All organizations have elements of each. What are the major influences in your organization? Is the balance appropriate? If not, what should be done? The measures referred to here will give you a quick check. Why not collect information from others and discuss the results? That could be the beginning of designing a particular survey for your own organization.

What are the key factors you feel should be included in a survey of staff opinion?

_____

_____

_____

_____

Outline three of the key questions you would ask and the way you would invite people to respond.

_____

_____

_____

Think of the "best" organization or "division" you have worked in. Outline below what were the major things you liked:

_____

_____

_____

_____

Now think of the "worst" organization or "division" you have worked in. This time describe the main things you disliked:

_____

_____

_____

_____

Now how does your current organization compare? What are the things you can influence or change? Points for action:

_____

_____

_____

_____

NOTES

1. Likert, R., *The Human Organization* (New York: McGraw-Hill, 1966).
2. Litwin, G.H., and Stringer, R.A., *Motivation and Organizational Climate* (Cambridge, Mass.: Harvard University Press, 1968).

CHAPTER 10

How do you learn?

HOW TO LEARN BY ANALOGY

MANAGING IS A CONTINUAL learning process. By definition, the manager's task involves dealing with non-routine problems. The manager is paid to organize work which is not totally systemized. In short, the manager has to learn each day how to manage the problems which emerge. This is what makes managing so interesting, yet so frustrating.

If we do not understand how we learn, it is difficult to organize learning opportunities for others. For those of us in the training and development profession, it is, therefore, important to have simple models which can guide our practice. The trouble is that most of the theories on learning that have been put forward are expressed in jargon. It is difficult, therefore, to use these immediately as practical aids to guide our planning and action.

I have found it more useful to look at the design of learning using a simple analogy. The analogy in question centers on *the game of golf*. I believe it illustrates some fundamental ideas about how we can design effective learning environments. In particular, it points to the "training mix" that we need to have if we are to improve people's performance.

Here I have outlined some of the fundamental ways in which people can learn to play golf. By inference, we can then translate these steps into training events which could be used in industry and commerce to help individuals improve their effectiveness. The model on the next page shows a number of specific behaviors that people engage in when playing golf.

Learning by Experience

Clearly, one can learn a lot by going out onto the golf course and playing eighteen holes. Essentially, it will be learning by doing. No doubt there will be a number of good shots mixed with a number of bad shots in any round of golf. From such activity, we can certainly learn what we

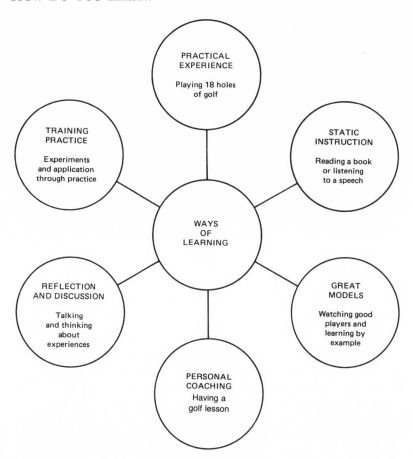

should not be doing, although it won't always tell us positively what we should be doing.

This approach is subject, therefore, to a great deal of trial and error. However, when all is said and done, there is no substitute for direct experience. The practical problems that one confronts force one to think through and try out new ideas.

Clearly, the parallel to this is learning on the job. Actually working through the problems which are confronted on a daily basis provides many learning opportunities. It is the way most of us learn most of the time. However, it can be costly. The cost in golf terms is probably a high score, but in the office and in the factory the cost can be more substantial.

While there is no substitute for learning on the job, it needs to be backed up with a considerable range of other learning experiences, both prior to and during one's work experience. In this way, we reduce trial and error. Let us look at some of these other opportunities.

Static Instruction

One can learn a lot about both golf and work from reading and listening. Both approaches involve us in a passive role. We are imbibing knowledge from other people on the assumption that we can transfer this into practice.

A good lecture or a good book can clear our mind on some of the essential things to do. However, such learning does not mean that we will be able to implement the ideas. There are many people who are extremely knowledgeable about golf yet who have never been able to master the game in practice. So it is in work situations. Some of the best teachers are not necessarily particularly good managers. People who are adept at training apprentices would not necessarily make first-class craftsmen. Static instruction, therefore, is useful as part of the training mix. It needs, however, to be linked very closely to the other elements which are described in the model, and in particular to the opportunity for practice and application, whether it be on the golf course or at work.

Observing Great Models

We can all learn a lot by watching other people. Usually, it is a pleasant form of learning, in that one does not have to do too much. It is a fairly passive form of discovery.

However, it can be extremely useful to watch the great players. Seeing how Jack Nicklaus, Tom Watson, or Lee Trevino addresses the golf ball can be a salutary form of instruction. We see them do things which we have never tried. We are encouraged by their example, in that they show what can be done, even if it is just a little outside our reach.

So it is at work. People, particularly lower down in the

hierarchy, are always watching and observing the behavior of those in senior positions. They observe both the good and the bad points. The important thing is that people at all levels act as models from whom we can learn.

The boss does not always realize just how important his own behavior is as a learning vehicle for his subordinates. They may well learn to imitate the things which he does successfully. Equally, they may learn to avoid behaviors which he adopts. Whatever goes on serves as a basis for understanding and as a guide to measure one's own performance.

We need better models in industry and commerce. It comes down to simple things such as chairing meetings, handling negotiations, coaching effectively, writing clear reports, and other fundamentals. If senior people are giving the lead and showing how it can be done, this is a powerful form of learning which others can observe and build upon.

Personal Coaching

Let us go back to our golf analogy and look at a more active form of learning. Typically, when things are not going too well, the amateur golfer will go along to the professional and ask for a lesson. We, therefore, move into a situation of active coaching.

The professional golfer will ask the amateur to play a few shots, and he will make comments and guide on the basis of what he sees. He will then ask you to play some more shots based upon his advice. In short, we have a planned approach to improvement. After each shot, the professional will make comments, either to reinforce what has been done or to correct what he thinks should not be done. It is an active approach to development.

Likewise, in the work situation there are many opportunities for managers to coach and guide their staff. Rather than being passive models, they can take an active role in working with their staff to improve performance. Naturally, this requires skill and empathy. Well-meant advice at the wrong time can be seen as interference and imposition.

However, well-organized coaching is a most powerful

form of learning. It means, in practice, talking through with subordinates how they conducted a negotiation, or reflecting upon their most recent report, so they get feedback to guide their subsequent efforts. It is important that the manager indicates what he is doing rather than doing it in a roundabout way. The manager, like the golf professional, should indicate that this is the time for coaching, although it is unlikely that he will do it in the same way, and certainly not on a shot-by-shot basis. Nevertheless, time spent coaching is rarely wasted. The problem is that we have too few people with the time or the skill to make a real success of it. It is an area where managers themselves need to do a lot of learning.

Reflection and Discussion

A considerable amount is learned by golfers while drinking at the bar. This is not so much because of the drinking but because of the discussion. Tales of woe are told of how greatness was nearly achieved. In the process, ideas are raised about what could be done next time. I believe that in the very act of reflection and discussion people are learning a great deal.

It is important to reflect upon experience, so that we can consider what to do next time. This is equally true at work and after a game of golf. In my experience, however, we are so busy going on to the next task at work that we rarely have time to talk through what we learned from the last one. The danger is that we may repeat the errors once again.

If reflection and discussion are vital to the learning process, and I believe they are, then increasingly we must make time for it to happen. To extend our golfing analogy, we must have a structure (equivalent to the bar) which makes it legitimate to talk about what we have learned from work. The parallels, I believe, are things like workshops, team development meetings, position review papers, and development meetings. The characteristic feature of these events is that there is no formal set agenda. The aim is not to discuss business matters as such, but to look at the process by which business has been conducted and could be improved. This requires someone who is prepared to act as a catalyst. Increasingly, people in the training and management development field are becoming active in facilitating such work. We need many more managers who are prepared to do it on a regular basis, as an integral part of their managerial work. In this way, we can articulate ideas based upon experience to guide future activity.

"Practice Makes Perfect"

The old saying has a lot going for it. Great golfers spend hours and hours practicing. They will go out to the practice ground and try out new ideas, as well as reinforcing existing skills. There is no substitute for developing one's skill, other than putting all the ideas derived from static instruction, watching others, coaching, and discussion into action. However, before doing it in a real match, it is important to get it right through practice.

The analogy holds for business. We can talk about learning, but the important thing is actual behavior. Clearly, we do not wish to take too many initial risks in the work situation. We need, therefore, more and more practice grounds. Action learning increasingly provides the focus for such work. Staff members are given small projects on which they can try out their skills and learn fundamental points without too much being at risk. We need to extend the opportunity for such control practice. Of course, the practice needs to be related directly to the work that people will be doing. It is no use practicing one thing and then doing another.

REVIEW YOUR OWN LEARNING

The forms of learning on page 130 apply to managerial work. How far do these methods enable you to learn the managerial job? Consider your own job during the last few months, and assess how far you have learned to improve your performance on the factors mentioned.

	Very little	Small amount	Moderate amount	Quite a lot	Great deal
(a) Experience (doing the job)					
(b) Instruction (talks, memos, letters, and books)					
(c) Comparison (observing others in action)					
(d) Coaching (on-job guidance through discussion)					
(e) Thinking and discussion (reflection, discussion, and action)					
(f) Testing (practice on budgets, plans, and projects)					

How do you plan to continue your learning during the next year? First of all, indicate the key things you feel you should concentrate on, and alongside in the space provided list the learning approaches you feel need to be used.

Key Areas for Learning   **Most Appropriate Method**

_____   _____

_____   _____

_____   _____

_____   _____

_____   _____

_____   _____

ACTION

What action do you now intend to take? If your plan involves planned coaching, who will act as your coach? If you are going to increase experimental testing, what does that mean in practice? It is useful to outline these as an aide-mémoire, so that you can review progress over the year.

Action Planned	Learning Method

It is useful to discuss such a checklist with someone else. This can be one's boss, the training manager, or someone whose counsel you value and who gives you room to develop your own personal thoughts. Writing things down is only the basis for discussion and action.

It may be difficult to start by writing down what your development needs are in any particular area. If you are in a new job, then it is often hard to see what is required of you. In such instances, it is important to talk with those who do have experience of the work. Clearly, your predecessor would be a useful contact. However, people in the other departments, whom you service or who provide a service to you, can be a good guide. Why not ask your subordinates? They invariably know where their previous boss "got it right" and where he "got it wrong." In short, conduct a diagnosis.

Once this has been done, you can then decide how far you intend to learn as you go, or learn in a more formal way, such as taking a course, reading a book, or similar approaches.

The important thing is developing an action plan. Don't expect to learn the key things in a new area, say, finance, within a few days. The process will follow the normal learning curve. The important thing is to find the time in your job to reflect on what you do. Reflection on experience is the key to successful development.

CHAPTER 11

What does managerial effectiveness mean?

CAN WE AGREE ON WHAT EFFECTIVE MANAGEMENT MEANS?

WE ALL KNOW what it is like to work with somebody who is ineffective. There are continual problems. Things don't get done on time, and there are often arguments. On many occasions, we feel somewhat embarrassed because it is difficult to confront people with their ineffectiveness. We try to give them clues and hints. If they don't take these clues, then we find it difficult to get our own work done.

It is important, therefore, in looking at what an effective manager is, to consider what an *ineffective* manager is. There is a need to be clear about the positive and negative aspects of the job.

Effectiveness implies that one behaves appropriately to the needs of the situation. However, this does not tell us very much. We need to be more precise if we are to learn what we need to do. Now managing essentially means working with a group of people in such a way that they can achieve things that they could not do working by themselves. Therefore, one aspect of effectiveness must reside in the relationships that a manger sets up and how he conducts those relationships. In addition, effectiveness needs to take into account how far the manager himself is technically competent and knowledgeable about the job that he is doing. It is these two key aspects of the personnel relations and the technical aspects which need to be looked at.

MANAGERS WE HAVE KNOWN

Let us consider what we mean by managerial effectiveness. Each one of us has worked for a number of managers. We have watched what they have done. Sometimes we have admired their actions and sometimes criticized them. By implication, we are making judgments about how effective they were.

Therefore, let us start a consideration of managerial effectiveness by looking at our own experience. Later, we shall look at the research work which has been done in the area of managerial effectiveness. The next exercise therefore provides a good base upon which to assess the practical value of such research.

On page 136 are two columns, and you are invited to put into the spaces provided comments relating to managers you have known. Please try to be specific in the comments that you make. If you are saying that one of your managers was effective because he "communicated," please say exactly *what* he did that you regarded as effective communication. Everybody communicates, but some people do it better than others, and we need to identify what it is that they do.

COMPARISONS OF MANAGERIAL EFFECTIVENESS

Drawing upon one's personal experience is a valuable guide. However, it is important to share this experience with others. Do other people regard those things that you have called effective behaviors in the same way you do? Likewise, do they feel the points that you have called ineffective are supported by their own experience?

It is useful, therefore, to meet in small groups to share and compare this information. Clearly, if there is a high degree of unanimity among the members in the group, then it lends support to the view that there is some overall agreement as to what an effective manager does. In particular, it should give some guidance to us on the things that we should avoid doing, as well as the things that we should positively seek to do.

At this point, it is useful, therefore, to look at one's own approach to managing. What are the key areas within which you are effective? Where do you need to put more effort and reduce your ineffectiveness?

On page 137, there is an opportunity to note your own perceptions regarding your effectiveness.

P.S. What do you intend to do differently in the next three months?

Managers who were ineffective in their performance behaved as follows:	Managers who were effective in their performance behaved as follows:

I consider that I am insufficiently effective in performing the following activities and behaviors:	I consider that I am reasonably effective in performing the following activities and behaviors:

ASPECTS OF MANAGERIAL EFFECTIVENESS

Looking at our own approach to managerial effectiveness and comparing it with others is a useful way of understanding. Yet, it is subjective, and we need now to look at what research studies have said about managerial effectiveness. Over the years, there has been a vast number of such studies. It is not our intention here to review all these. However, it is important just to identify some of the major pieces of work, so that we see the context of our own personal assessment.

One of the major studies conducted at Ohio University (Fleishman[1]) suggested that there are two factors which managers need to pay attention to:

1. The organizational arrangements whereby a manager structured group activities, provided resources, set up schedules, and planned the activities to achieve the task at hand; and
2. Personal considerations, whereby a manager set up good relationships between people and worked in such a way as to help individuals develop their own personal needs in the context of the work that had to be done.

These have been referred to previously (Chapter 6) as task orientation and relationship orientation.[2] Korman[3] found low correlations in performance among managers who were high in both the above factors. However, there were high correlations for those who had high consideration for staff and for the job satisfaction expressed by those people. Nevertheless, it has been noted that where there is high pressure for production, those who stress task factors do tend to get more productivity.

Many other studies build upon this original dichotomy. More recently, Fiedler[4] has emphasized that there are three things a manager needs to know before he can decide how to behave effectively.

(a) Are the relationships between the leader and the members favorable or unfavorable?
(b) Is the task highly structured and routine or demanding a high degree of creativity and innovation?
(c) Is the leader's position power based upon his organizational authority strong or weak?

Fiedler has argued that where the leader's relationships are good, where the task is highly structured, and where the leader has high authority, then the manager can afford to be task-oriented and authoritative. However, where there are poor relationships, a complex task, and a low degree of authority, then it is likely he will have to become more democratic.

EXPECTATIONS A KEY FACTOR

In addition to all this, my colleague Richard Glube[5] has indicated that *empathy* seems to play a major part in managerial success. His research indicates that managers who had higher-producing groups, where job satisfaction was also higher than average, were able to adjust their style based upon a reading of the situation.

There is substantial evidence to indicate that the early experience a man has within an organization can influence his future development to a substantial degree. Berlew and Hall[6] have shown that the first year a man spends with the company can substantially influence his progress within the next five years. They found that there was a .72 correlation between how much a company expects of a man in his first year and how much he contributes during the next five years. They stressed that the first year is critical, in so far as the individual adopts positive job attitudes and high standards. They conclude that it should follow that "a new manager who meets the challenge of one highly demanding job will be given subsequently a more demanding job and his level of contribution will rise as he responds to the company's growing expectations of him."

In short, the expectations that are set in the early days of a man's managerial career, by his boss and other influential people in the company, have considerable impact on future behavior. This has been shown conclusively in other fields in a classic experiment by Rosenthal and Jacobson.[7] They informed school teachers that as a result of a test, certain of their pupils had high development potential. In fact, the students had been selected at random. However, when the students were tested at a later date, it was found that the students who had been nominated by Rosenthal and Jacobson had improved their performance significantly more than those not so nominated. They concluded that the teachers had conveyed high expectations to the students, and that the students had responded by fulfilling these expectations. This effect has become known as the *self-fulfilling prophecy*. In short, there are conditions where a person can develop his performance, because he is convinced that others whom he respects expect him to do so and support him in his endeavors.

The results of work conducted with industrial managers support the ideas and work of those in education. Furthermore, Fleishman[8] has noted one positive finding on the determinance of leadership style was that the supervisor tends to behave as his boss does.

In a review of the amazing effects that expectations can have on the development of people, J. Stirling Livingstone[9] summarized the major findings, as follows:

(a) What a manager expects of his subordinates and the way he treats them largely determine their performance and career progress.

(b) A unique characteristic of superior managers is their ability to create high performance expectations that subordinates fulfill.

(c) Less effective managers fail to develop similar expectations, and as a consequence the productivity of their subordinates suffers.

(d) Subordinates more often than not appear to do what they believe they are expected to do.

WHAT DO SUBORDINATES LOOK FOR?

The above comments give us general guidance, but it is important to have some specific indication of what people have found helpful. In a major study by Scott Myers,[10] which involved 806 managers, there is a clear indication that the behavior of the boss is seen by subordinates to have an effect on their motivation. Myers concluded that effective management

(a) enables individuals to achieve personal goals by achieving organizational goals;

(b) is managed by the individual (rather than managing the individual) in the achievement of goals; and

(c) reflects the developmental philosophy of supervision.

Here is a summary of the key points:

Items mentioned mainly by people who saw their boss as a person who motivated them:	Percent agreeing	Items mentioned mainly by people who were poorly motivated by their managers:	Percent agreeing
(a) Easy to talk to even when under pressure	80+	You have to pick carefully the time when you talk to him	50+
(b) Tries to see the merit in your ideas even if they conflict with his	90+	Because he's the boss, he tends to assume his ideas are best	40+

Items mentioned mainly by people who saw their boss as a person who motivated them:	Percent agreeing	Items mentioned mainly by people who were poorly motivated by their managers:	Percent agreeing
(c) Tries to help his people understand company objectives	80+	Lets his people figure out for themselves how company objectives apply to them	50+
(d) Tries to give his people all the information they want	60+	Provides his people with as much information as he thinks they need	70+
(e) Consistent high expectations of subordinates	80+	His expectations of subordinates can be very changeable from day to day	50+
(f) Tries to encourage people to reach out in new directions	80+	Tries to protect his people from taking big risks	50+
(g) Takes your mistakes in stride so long as you can learn from them	90+	Allows little room for mistakes, especially those that might embarrass him	50+
(h) Tries mainly to correct mistakes and figure out how they can be prevented in the future	90+	When something goes wrong, tries primarily to find out who caused it	40+
(i) Expects superior performance and gives credit when you do it	80+	Expects you to do an adequate job; doesn't say much unless something goes wrong	60+

While there was some overlap between these responses, it is clear that the highly motivated managers do have a positive view of how their boss seeks to help them. Those who were poorly motivated clearly thought the boss was somewhat constraining and did not trust them. These are key indications to all of us on what subordinates expect from the above. This is as important as what the boss expects from the subordinate.

SMOOTHING THE PATH

The work of House[11] suggests that:

1. Leaders are likely to have satisfied subordinates if they are able to and do reward subordinates' work which achieves the set standards required.
2. The satisfaction of subordinates is likely to increase if leaders can clarify the link between achieving goals and receiving rewards by coaching and direction.
3. A leader can help the satisfaction of subordinates by supporting them in difficult work and making the task easier to accomplish.
4. The leader can make employees more satisfied by reducing the frustration and pressure of work.

Leadership is not easy to define. We do, however, usually know it when we see it. For those of us interested in improving our leadership abilities, it is important to reflect upon what others have said. However, knowing what leadership is about does not mean that we shall necessarily become more effective. This demands practice and action.

Therefore, in concluding this section let us identify those things that we feel we must concentrate upon if we are to be more effective. The chart on the next pages indicates the areas wherein we can develop leadership effectiveness. This will involve becoming more knowledgeable and establishing improved relationships with others. It is useful as a checklist to guide our thinking and action.

Areas for development	What is success?	How is it achieved?

Finance

1 _____

_____

2 _____

_____

3 _____

_____

4 _____

Production

1 _____

_____

2 _____

_____

3 _____

_____

4 _____

Marketing/Sales

1 _____

_____

2 _____

_____

3 _____

_____

4 _____

Areas for development	What is success?	How is it achieved?

Personnel/Industrial Relations

1 _____

2 _____

3 _____

4 _____

Research

1 _____

2 _____

3 _____

4 _____

Personal

1 _____

2 _____

3 _____

4 _____

NOTES

1. Fleishman, E.A., "Twenty Years of Consideration and Structure," *Current Developments in the Study of Leadership,* edited by Fleishman, E.A., and Hunt, J.G. (Carbondale, Ill.: Southern Illinois University Press, 1973).

2. Blake, R., and Mouton, J., *The Managerial Grid* (Houston: Gulf Publishing Co., 1964).

3. Korman, A., "Consideration, Initiating Structure and Organisational Criteria—A Review," *Personnel Psychology,* Vol. 19, 1966.

4. Fiedler, F., et al., *Improving Leadership Effectiveness* (New York: John Wiley, 1976).

5. Glube, R., "Leadership and Decision Making," unpublished doctoral dissertation, Cranfield Institute of Technology, Cranfield, England, 1978.

6. Berlew, D., and Hall, D., "The Socialization of Managers," *Administrative Science Quarterly,* September 1976.

7. Rosenthal, R., and Jacobson, L., *Pygmalion in the Classroom* (New York: Holt, Rinehart & Winston, 1968).

8. Fleishman, E.A., "Leadership Climate, Human Relations Training and Supervisory Behaviour," in *Personnel Psychology,* No. 6, 1953.

9. Livingstone, J.S., "Pygmalion in Management," *Harvard Business Review,* July 1969.

10. Myers, C.S., "Conditions for Manager Motivation," *Harvard Business Review,* January 1966.

11. House, R., "The Path-Goal Theory of Leader Effectiveness," *Administrative Science Quarterly,* Vol. 16, Dec. 1971.

Index

147